THE 100-Mile Walk

THE 100-Mile Walk

A FATHER AND SON ON A QUEST TO
FIND THE ESSENCE OF LEADERSHIP

Sander A. Flaum and Jonathon A. Flaum

with Mechele Flaum

Foreword by John Glenn

AMACOM

AMERICAN MANAGEMENT ASSOCIATION

New York · Atlanta · Brussels · Chicago · Mexico City
San Francisco · Shanghai · Tokyo · Toronto · Washington, D.C.

Special discounts on bulk quantities of AMACOM books are
available to corporations, professional associations, and other
organizations. For details, contact Special Sales Department,
AMACOM, a division of American Management Association,
1601 Broadway, New York, NY 10019.
Tel.: 212-903-8316. Fax: 212-903-8083.
Website: www.amacombooks.org

*This publication is designed to provide accurate and authoritative
information in regard to the subject matter covered. It is sold with
the understanding that the publisher is not engaged in rendering
legal, accounting, or other professional service. If legal advice or other
expert assistance is required, the services of a competent professional
person should be sought.*

Library of Congress Cataloging-in-Publication Data

Flaum, Sander A., 1937-
    The 100-mile walk : a father and son on a quest to find the essence of leadership /
Sander A. Flaum and Jonathon A. Flaum with Mechele Flaum ; foreword by John Glenn.
        p.   cm.
    Includes bibliographical references and index.
    ISBN 0-8144-0863-X (hardcover)
    1. Leadership.   I. Title: One hundred mile walk.   II. Flaum, Jonathon A.,
1968–   III. Flaum, Mechele, 1950–   IV. Title.

HD57.7.F593   2006
303.3' 4—dc22

                                                                2005020263

Printing number

10   9   8   7   6   5   4   3   2   1

CONTENTS

FOREWORD

The Leadership Enigma

My dad told me stories of his service in the First World War in France, and my hometown of New Concord, Ohio, resembled the one in the famed Broadway hit *The Music Man.* There was not a better place to grow up in America. Because of my father, the warmth and purpose of the people of New Concord, and a great high school civics teacher, the desire to serve my country found its way into my heart early and burns as brightly today as it ever did.

When we founded the John Glenn Institute for Public Service and Public Policy at the Ohio State University in 1998, our vision was to create a place where young people could be inspired to public service the way I was years ago. After a life in the military, NASA, and the United States Senate, I knew that there was still much work to be done. Who would be our next generation of leaders? Who would train and inspire them? How would they know that public service is not only an honor but a great joy? I wanted to build a place that grappled with these questions and was prepared to develop innovative responses to them. I am proud to say that in the years since founding the institute, we have made great strides down this road—though a long way is left to travel.

When Sander and Jonathon asked me to talk to them about this book, I told them that I don't know any more about leadership than anyone else. I know there are shelves full of books on the subject—I read many of them starting from the time I was in the Marine Corps—but still, the subject feels like a great mystery to me. I was relieved to hear that it was a mystery to Sander and Jonathon too, because sometimes struggling with our questions is more important than trying to present neatly packaged answers. As this father and son team persisted, I decided to get involved for two reasons.

The first reason is that this book does not presume answers; it asks probing questions. It analyzes real-life leaders from different walks of life who are acting as leaders out in the field. Not simply the well-known leaders either, but those folks just making things happen every day. This is not a book about the beliefs of leadership; it is a book about how real people practice leadership in a variety of circumstances. I think this is the only way to understand the leadership enigma, to study the practices of real leaders.

The second reason, and probably the most compelling one, is that this book is written by a father and son of very different generations and points of view. The book models its own message that leaders from the next generation must step up and take an active role. I make no bones about the fact that I want to inspire young people to get involved in public service leadership positions. I want them to understand the joys, duties, and rewards of such an endeavor.

This book speaks to young people. It invites them to develop their own leadership practice. It is a call to action for them without being a diatribe. This book illustrates what I aim to do with young people every day—to hold a dialogue. The book puts the older generation and younger generation in discussion together for the purpose of discovering what qualities make someone a good leader. We need to ask these questions together. We need to make a space for every age and generation to lead together, and understand each other, so we can fulfill missions that are bigger than ourselves.

When I orbited the earth that first time, I was struck by how fragile the atmosphere is—how precious the whole earthly experience is for us. The feeling of that orbit has never left me. Our responsibility to serve and lead is awesome. If this next generation is not inspired and prepared, we are in big trouble. May this book serve as a guidepost to a life of leadership in which the mission is always about something bigger—something further out there beyond the horizon.

—JOHN GLENN

ACKNOWLEDGMENTS

FROM SANDER

*Some luck lies in not getting what you thought
you wanted but getting what you have, which once
you have got it you may be smart enough to see is
what you would have wanted had you known.*
—GARRISON KEILLOR

The vision for this book rose out of my intense curiosity about the activity of leadership . . . whatever *leadership* really means. As John Glenn writes in the foreword, I'm not sure I can ever define the term *leadership;* but I sure can describe it when I see it executed by other people. I am privileged to have been mentored and surrounded by some wonderful, wonderful people who are profiled in this book. They have taught me, my students, Jonathon, and Mechele how people are inspired, how passion is instilled, and how great executions are manifested. The people we have written about and studied are people who have accomplished much in their lives for their firms, for their cities, for their universities, and for the people who have been privileged to work with them and for them.

My deep thanks to Jonathon and Mechele, who helped me so much to think, write, and express my thoughts on leadership and who made laughter part of the big deliverables.

Getting back to Garrison Keillor and his description of luck, I am grateful that I have wonderful children in Pamela and Jonathon and am surrounded by their loving (and brilliant) children. I found later in my life an extraordinary human being who is supportive and loving, my wonderful wife, Mechele. Without her inspiration, logic, and support, *The 100-Mile Walk* would never have been written.

Also, I would like to thank Adrienne Hickey, our very talented editor at AMACOM, and her excellent colleagues, particularly development editor Barry Richardson; and Florence Stone, editorial director of marketing communications for the American Management Association. My hat is off as well to a great leader at AMA, Bob Smith.

The book focuses in the main on the speakers at the Fordham Leadership Forum. I am indebted to former Dean Ernest Scalberg and ex-President Reverend Joseph O'Hare for recruiting me to start the Leadership Forum at Fordham. I salute the present dean of Business, Dr. Sharon Smith, and, of course, Reverend Joseph M. McShane, president of Fordham University, one of my mentors, and a man I respect greatly. Lastly, thanks to my book agents, Jan Miller and Michael Broussard of Dupree-Miller & Associates, for their understanding and belief in this book concept and for all they did to get our first book published by the folks at AMACOM.

FROM JONATHON

After finishing this book, I went with my wife, Tami, and our son, Ren, to Yellowstone National Park. During the drive from the airport in Salt Lake up to Wyoming, it struck me that we had packed everything except our binoculars. I vowed to buy a pair before entering the park, but I forgot. And then, lo and behold, we saw more wildlife in that one week than my wife and I had ever seen in two seasons of working there years ago. We drove past a bald eagle's nest every day on our way into the park from our cabin, spotted black and grizzly bear within 200 feet, and saw huge herds of bison, loads of bull elk, and even pronghorn sheep all perfectly observed with the naked eye.

On the last night of our trip, back in our hotel in Salt Lake, I dreamt that I looked in my backpack and found my binoculars. I woke up wondering what our trip would have been like if I had had the binoculars—would the wildlife have stayed away?

Writing this book, I didn't need binoculars. Everybody came close to show me the way. The leaders were all so forthcoming with their stories that they made my job easy. Our editor at AMACOM, Adrienne Hickey, provided critical insights that opened things up. Her forthrightness saved us time and effort. My stepmom, Mechele, is a tour de force—her attention to detail and refinement is unparalleled. She stepped up to help us manage and edit this project with a no-nonsense strength that propelled us forward to completion.

My father let me into his world and made it accessible to me. He put his self in plain sight so that I didn't have to strain to see him. Such a gift belies description.

The vision to see what is most important in life that my wife, Tami, gives me is beyond reckoning. Finally, I want to acknowledge my son, Ren, who continues to teach me what it means to be a father and thereby, a son.

THE 100-Mile Walk

PROLOGUE

Walking the Rocky Road

FROM SANDER

There are 250 books on leadership written every year. It's a pretty popular topic. I've read a lot of them, particularly by those CEOs who have made it big and whom I personally admire, such as Jack Welch and Larry Bossidy. As a former CEO of a large multinational company, I've learned much from them.

I also read books by educators such as Warren Bennis, Peter Drucker, and Noel Tichy. Their writings, in the main, are directed to the Old Guys like myself or, better put, Old Guys writing to Old Guys.

The challenge I've always faced with relating the wisdom of these well-known leadership practitioners to my twenty- and thirty-something MBA students is that their lessons really don't apply to my students' present situations. That's what made me decide to write a book for both twenty- and thirtysomethings and forty- to sixty-somethings on achieving a leader's role and how contemporary leaders deal with the issues of leading.

This is a book about hard work and sacrifice. After reading about the great leaders discussed here, you may very well choose not to move ahead with your vision of running the company or the union or becoming editor-in-chief or getting to the top of your organization. But if hard work and sacrifice fit your personality and lifestyle, you'll be considerably better prepared than your competitors to anticipate and survive, and get satisfaction from leading.

I wrote this book to expose the insights, the demeanor, the personality, and the character traits of people who are admired by their people as leaders. I view them not simply through my senior corporate CEO eyes, but through the eyes of my inquisitive MBA students as well. You will also hear from my son Jonathon at the end of each chapter. Jonathon is a thirty-six-year-old entrepreneur and student of Zen who teaches me more about a new way of doing business in these polarizing times than any case study ever could.

As you read on, you'll quickly see that there's no "one size fits all" leadership. However, you will also quickly pick up that all of our leader-heroes have, in some fashion, inculcated a certain ethic into their psyche and gut. What they work on and practice every day is what you need to practice and work on every day, too. Yes, it's hard work. Is it worth all this energy, focus, sweat, and sacrifice to reach the top? Only you can be the judge of that. I do hope that after reading this book, you give it a shot.

Every generation and personality leads in its own way; and my premise is that to progress together, we have to lead with each other in mind. At best, we can only approximate what makes leaders perform brilliantly under pressure by studying the *practices* they incorporate into their leadership zeitgeist. Let's start with a short profile of Jonathon and me. Typical of the older and younger generations at work, we have a lot of differences, yet we need to find a way to blend, if we are going to get the work done.

PROFILE:
Older Leader/Younger Leader

	Sander A. Flaum (SAF)	Jonathon A. Flaum (JAF)
Political affiliation	Republican	Independent
Religious affiliation	Jewish	Zen Buddhist
Residence	New York City	Asheville, North Carolina
Most influential book	*Execution* by Larry Bossidy and Ron Charam	*Walden* by H. D. Thoreau
Clothes	Ralph Lauren	Gap
Ideal vacation	Golf in Scottsdale	Backcountry roam in Yellowstone N.P.
Age	65	36
Formative experience	U.S. Army	Traveling solo around USA on Greyhound bus
Advanced degrees	MBA–Marketing	MA–Philosophy of Religion, MFA–Theater
Leadership heroes	Winston Churchill, Abraham Lincoln, Colin Powell	Shunryu Suzuki, Martin Luther King, Jr., Gandhi
First section gone for in Sunday *Times*	Business	Arts and Leisure
Vehicle	Audi	Subaru
Number of suits in closet	22	3
Favorite drink	Absolut and Tonic	Pint of Guinness
Thing to do when not driving the car	Prepare for next meeting	Nap
Years it took to be CEO	20	1
Favorite dog	Boxer	Boxer
Number of states resided	3	8
Favorite breakfast	Bagel/cream cheese with pickled lox on the side	Bagel/cream cheese with pickled lox on the side
Fear of flying	No	Yes
Title	CEO, Flaum Partners, former chairman, and CEO Euro RSCG Life Becker	CEO, WriteMind Communications

In putting this book together, I saw that my son, my students, and my young employees looked like me in their business suits, but underneath, they were very different individuals. More and more, I saw evidence that generations and personality types working together under one roof were unbelievably different in their thinking about business, the paradigms of leadership, and life in general. How could the older generation invite the younger generation to lead if they didn't speak the same language?

Were we continually missing the point the other was trying to make? Jon and I got by that way for a long time, and we were father and son. I started thinking about Jon and some of the things he had challenged me on over the years—things I thought were just coming out of his philosophical weirdness that had no relevance to business. That was until Jon entered business and I realized corporations would be foolhardy not to want to attract talented people who could think, write, communicate, and lead like he did. Yet many of these selfsame institutions didn't have a clue about how to successfully approach and develop their Fortune 500 younger people.

I wasn't being touchy-feely by probing these questions, I was thinking about my business. There are new paradigms infusing our workplace (see facing chart), and older and younger leaders needed to be familiar with both sides of the coin or risk the big money, the big breakthroughs, getting left on the table.

I saw Jon and me as a metaphor for the problem. Jon's uncanny and natural leadership skills, eclectic interests, fearlessness, integrity, and ability to adapt were marks of what was great about his generation. My workaholic work ethic, "fight for a yes" stubbornness, creativity, stability, self-discipline, and toughness were the mark of mine. One generation and orientation needed the other, just like father and son need each other. Without a solid bond between the two, both are incomplete.

OLD PARADIGM

Increase revenue every quarter.

Few women are qualified for top jobs.

Competition builds successful teams.

Top-down management is best.

Respect seniority.

Dress for success.

Fit in.

Show company loyalty.

NEW PARADIGM

Tithe 10 percent of profits to charity.

Women are capable CEOs.

Collaboration builds successful teams.

Build consensus first, though the buck still stops at the top.

Encourage innovation from *all* levels.

Dress appropriately for comfort.

Be diverse.

Move on if recognition and growth opportunities are absent.

My goal was not to go off on an unbounded lecture from one generation to the other. It's too commonplace that a professor (or CEO) is up there rambling on, thinking everybody "gets it" as they feign interest, while actually what's going on is that they're waiting for the next class or the next paycheck. I wanted to make sure that wouldn't happen—and I trusted my son would help me, question me, and keep me honest.

OUR WALK, OUR TALK, AND THE WRITING PROCESS

Like the old Native American proverb, we would walk a mile in the other's moccasins. I would walk fifty miles with Jon on his favorite trails, with him leading, and he would walk fifty miles with me in the places of my choosing. I didn't own a pair of hiking shoes when we started and Jon didn't own golf shoes. We agreed to finish the hundred miles no matter what.

It's Jonathon's role in the book to share his perspective on my narrative from his personal vantage point and in light of his generation's perspective. Each chapter to follow will be my narrative on a particular leadership practice followed by Jonathon's "younger leader" perspective on it.

To write this book, I took the interviews and lectures of a remarkable group of Fordham Leadership Forum guest speakers and some other exemplary leaders I admire and I studied them with Jon. Jon also came to New York City to attend some of the lectures, contacted many of the Forum leaders for in-depth follow-up interviews, and talked with leaders outside the Forum. In our 100-mile trek, we went to New Orleans so we could eat great food and hear great music while working on leadership. We spent time together walking in Manhattan so that we could be around the high energy of so many of the great leaders we had studied. We went to upstate New York where we could hike in a place we used to go when we were younger. We went out to Bridgehampton, New York, so we could golf together and walk on the beach and talk leadership. We spent a bit of time in Columbus, Ohio (you'll find out why). And finally, we went to Asheville, North Carolina, so we could hike through the Blue Ridge Mountains and continue to let the leadership dialogue unfold.

We spent six months talking leadership, dissecting differences, exploring nuances, and growing closer. Truth is that this dialogue and appreciation between older and younger is bogus if you can't do it at home. And Jonathon and I couldn't for a long time. I had a personal impetus to write this book as much as a professional one. Confession: For all our process maps, pie charts, quarterly reports, and mission statements, we business folk are still primarily ruled and lead by emotion. My efforts to "get human" with my son taught me firsthand that there are different ways to judge success for all people and that bringing those ways to the table makes us better people. And being a businessperson, always in search of hidden values, I discovered an incredible residual benefit to this openness—seeking to understand also makes us much better businesspeople.

We walked a lot. On the surface, it comes off as some extracurricular fun, but in reality, the walk changed my life. People should walk together; managers should walk with their direct reports, women with men, the twenty-five-year-old technological whiz with the fifty-two-year-old CFO. Walking together, we learn the gifts that the other possesses and, in turn, take the time to rediscover our own gifts. It worked for us. We hope it works for you.

A NOTE TO YOU IN YOUR TWENTIES AND THIRTIES: MY MENTORS

You are a generation that deeply desires to do things your own way. You are the inheritors of dubious "corporate greatness" and have come out of college (or skipped it) with a much different view of leadership than your parents had. You have your own style, philosophies, favorite TV shows, books, music, restaurants, games, hobbies, and venues. You don't have many contemporary leaders to emulate though. You see the Achilles heels of leaders, as much if not more so than you do the mythological heroism they became famous for. You have a keen sense of awareness and realism about the world. You do not trust quickly. Are not easily won over and are painfully aware that leaders have feet of clay just as you do. It makes you an egalitarian group, a fair one, and an honest one.

But you need leaders too, and if you have picked up this book, very likely you are interested in leading yourself. But what do Jack Welch's or Larry Bossidy's books have to say to you? You feel skeptical of these corporate giants who grew up in a completely different generation and speak to that generation in their books. At the same time, you want to wade into the fray and make a difference and become a leader in your own right. How do you do it? Do you throw out the baby with the bathwater and simply make all new rules and find a new way to lead that is entirely your own? That was certainly my thought at twenty-two, but by the time I was thirty, that seemed all too arrogant and shortsighted.

Older leaders definitely have a great deal to teach you; but you have a great deal to teach them, too. Imagine if we can learn from each other, be open to hearing the other, and find a new synthesized paradigm for leadership? It would be awesome, and maybe even better than that, it would be inviting and inclusive—creating a space we can all live and work within together. I wrote this book with the encouragement of many folks to illustrate that this kind of dialogue could be mutually beneficial: my business and educational colleagues; my boomer, Gen X, and Gen Y employees; my MBA students; and many wonderful and talented leaders, some known but many unsung. The subject matter we will be debating and discussing is not "salute the general, keep your mouth shut, business as usual." New generations bring new life, new abilities, and new insights to the table. The door is open, and I want you very much to come in and get comfortable.

The leadership practices we will unpack in the book are meant not to rein you in; rather, they're presented here to help you air out your ideas and become the kind of leader *you* want to be.

When I talked to Jonathon about this idea, he brought up an eighth-century Zen master, Rinzai, who said, "The greatest truth is to be found outside the written dogma." I don't know much about Rinzai, but I agree with him. Set something in stone and it becomes petrified. These practices have to be alive, exhilarating, and vibrant. They have to have the ability to shift and rotate to accommodate the unpredictable demands of the never-been-seen-before present moment of your life. They are not admonitions, rules, or commandments brought down from the mount or corporate headquarters—they must be understood, embraced, and lived by you and you alone.

A NOTE TO MY CONTEMPORARIES

I'm a corporate lifer like a lot of you, and I've taught in graduate business schools for the past thirty-plus years. But I want to warn you: I didn't write this book to put out more of the traditional rhetoric that we have all heard in leadership workshops, confer-

> ## Jon:
>
> *Rinzai was known as Lin Chi in China and was the founder of the Sudden Enlightenment school of Ch'an Buddhism, which became known as Zen in Japan. Rinzai was famous for arduously urging his students to focus on their experience and not to substitute academic learning or study of scriptures for the truth of enlightenment, which he said can be received only through personal struggle and firsthand knowledge.*

ences, boardrooms, and annual meetings a thousand times. I wrote this book because if we do not keep pace with the young leaders waiting to emerge, we will lose the best and the brightest. I don't want that to happen, and knowing what I do about other lifetime workaholics like me, neither do you.

Even when I asked my friend, retired senator and astronaut John Glenn, about leadership, he told me: "I have no more insight on leadership than anybody else. There are shelves full of books on leadership, book after book after book that is required reading of Marine officers, but still there has always been something about leadership that is inherently mysterious to me."

DIALOGUES WITH REAL-WORLD LEADERS

To provide a useful anchor for younger women and men who choose to lead and a reference point for older executives, I've tried to ground this book in the "the horse's mouth" experience that came out of the widely respected Fordham Leadership Forum of the Fordham University Graduate School of Business, where I am founder and chair.

All quotes not otherwise attributed come from these lectures, follow-up interviews, and firsthand interviews with additional leaders whom Jonathon and I came in contact with. Because the book is based on real conversations between actual students and respected corporate, governmental, academic, and nonprofit leaders, I hope it will serve to push back at the traditional "I did it this way; you do it, too" words of wisdom put out by the usual group of leadership suspects.

We talked to folks like Thomas Von Essen, New York City fire commissioner during 9/11; Bill Toppeta, president of MetLife International; Faith Popcorn, futurist and marketing consultant to the Fortune 500; Nancy Lublin, founder of the venerable not-for-profit Dress for Success; Father Joseph O'Hare, former president of Fordham University; Reverend Joseph M. McShane, current Fordham president; Frances Hesselbein, chair of the Leader to Leader Institute, (formerly The Peter Drucker Foundation); Howard Safir, former New York City police commissioner; Jeff Rich, CEO of Affiliated Computer Services, Inc. (ACS); Senator John Glenn; and many other great leaders.

In most MBA management courses, professors assign case studies and students present analyses. The fact is that with a case study, you have all the data neatly packaged according to the Harvard Business School formula and the analysis becomes pretty staid. I did that for a long time, but I got to the point where I needed to do something different.

In real life, you have to gather whatever data is available and then use your instincts and intuitions, whatever you have in your bag. Those kinds of resources don't show up in textbooks or in stock analysts' reports; they're in the heads and guts of people who

ıders for a living. I believed that if my students could actu-
this process firsthand and were free to enter into a dialogue
wiтн a leader, it would be more than instructional; it would be real-
life learning in action—the inspired kind that prompts you to think
of new ideas, to try new things, even to change your life.

NINE LEADERSHIP PRACTICES

Leaders invited to the Fordham Leadership Forum tell us how
things really get accomplished, with no sugar coating. We are entrusted with their innermost reflections, views, practices, and most
important, their mistakes. From the speakers, the coursework, the
student feedback, my son's queries, and my own lifelong experience
as a student/practitioner of leadership, nine key leadership practices
emerged. For ease of memory and because business school students
love shorthand, I used the letter "P" to describe them.

The Nine Ps of Leadership

1. People
2. Purpose
3. Passion
4. Performance
5. Persistence
6. Perspective
7. Paranoia
8. Principles
9. Practice

The last one is the one that stops you . . . how do leaders
practice "practice"? Jonathon would describe this as a Zen koan: a

question to which there is no specific rational and objective answer, a question posed where you must discover the answer for yourself within the specific context of your own life. If this sounds a bit loosey-goosey to you Stephen Covey "7 Habits" types, don't worry . . . it did to me, too. But that's what this process is all about, being open to looking at old things in a new way and the reverse.

Jon:

There are no rational answers to certain questions. Certain questions demand "body and mind" answers—that is, the student does not "know" the answer, but rather becomes it.

The chapters that follow take each leadership practice and examine it from my perspective and experience, followed by a response from Jonathon, according to his perspective.

FROM JONATHON

When we started thinking about writing this book featuring Dad's generation's point of view in contrast to mine, I made him a proposal. I thought we should literally walk the walk as well as talk the talk, since walking already had a history with us, serving to open up new possibilities. I suggested we walk 100 miles together talking about the Ps of leadership and the people we believed best exemplified them. Dad was not a hiker. (His last big one was a twenty-miler in ninety-degree heat, with full pack, in the army.) He likes to tour and golf at nice resorts and to have his bed turned down.

But he agreed anyway. I thought it would be a great way for us to track down the bottom of the thing.

What intrigued me most about doing this book with my father was his willingness to openly question what he was putting out there to young people. Anytime someone acts all-knowing, I'm skeptical. I think self-analysis is a welcome trait for a leader to possess. Still, there are those leaders who think they need to present themselves as all-knowing so we in turn will follow them. And unfortunately, we often have, even if it was right over a moral or actual cliff. That's why for me, understanding leadership is extremely important, first, because we all are affected by our leaders and second, because we need to have the sound judgment to choose them wisely.

Personally, I have always been drawn first to the poet, artist, philosopher, and radical individualist who is vexed by the meaning and direction of his own life and committed to finding what is right and true, whether or not anybody follows him on the chosen path. So, as I share my perspective on my father's thoughts on leadership, my style will be markedly different. In addition to the leaders we interviewed, I will refer to poetry, philosophers, Zen stories, and religious leaders. For me, such references contain within them perennial issues central to leadership. By invoking such things we can, I hope, help to bring more perspective to the younger contemporary issues of leadership. This approach may feel discursive at times, but in the end, my father and I are trying to get at the central tenets of leadership each in our own way.

The reality, though, especially where leadership is concerned, is that there is always more than one narrative. There is not now, nor was there ever, a monologue about leadership, despite the utterings of the Napoleons and Caesars of the world. I speak for myself and, at times, I will try to speak for some in my generation. Not because I have some special authority, but because I am the appointed alternative representative and because I have interviewed and read numerous workplace generational experts—and because as Thoreau wrote in *Walden,* "I should not talk so much about myself if there were anybody else I knew as well."

Henry David Thoreau is a role model for me. *Walden* is a story I don't want to copy (Thoreau warned against that) but something I do try to emulate. Not just the communion with nature, but the individualism of "walking to the beat of my own drum." *Walden* is not a book only for the woods. I see it as a book for governments and business and for evaluating the busyness of our everyday personal lives. It is a text that bids us to slow down and take note of the "why" of our labor as much as contemplate the how and the what. Thoreau wrote of building a cabin and raising beans. Many of us instead spend our days writing white papers; preparing marketing strategies, spreadsheets, or legal briefs; building websites; or creating software. Thoreau would never ask us to quit our jobs and take up his. He asks us instead to pay attention to our work and bring deliberate care to it. Thoreau asks us to search out meaning in the mundane. He knows how difficult it is to stay in the moment and not race to the outcome. But when we practice just this, be we executives or farmers or accountants or software developers, we meet on the field of human life. And it is this human field that Thoreau was aiming to cultivate when *Walden* was first published 150 years ago.

I wanted to write this leadership book with my father so that the two of us could meet on the field of human life and encourage others to do the same. My own life in business came to fruition by happenstance; it was nothing I planned. I saw my father's world of business as wholly other. For my master's thesis in philosophy of religion, I worked on the poetry of Rainer Maria Rilke, a rather enigmatic and hermetic German poet of the early twentieth century. I focused on one particular cycle of his poems, the *Duino*

Elegies. Composed over a ten-year period, the elegies dramatize Rilke's mystical conversation with an angel that first called out to him on the cliffs of the castle at Duino. I analyzed the cycle from a philosophical perspective, treating Rilke as a religious mystic and the poems as his manifested tale of mystical experience. A part of the thesis was published in an anthology on Rilke when I was twenty-six. I've written stage plays, screenplays, a documentary, and a novel since, receiving my MFA in playwriting from the University of Southern California. I love the theater and have been recognized for my work, but never in a way that allowed me to pay the bills.

A PHILOSOPHER AND PLAYWRIGHT BECOMES A BUSINESSMAN

Knowing this about me, you would think I'd much rather sit down with a good work of fiction or a book on philosophy than pick up a book on business. So how did I end up starting my own business as a corporate speechwriter, speaker trainer, and ghostwriter, as well as an editorial consultant?

My story, I have come to find out, is far from atypical. In my travels and interviews (and through general curiosity), I have come to know many people like me in business—creative writers, former academics, artists, actors, teachers, all who fell into business by necessity and happenstance. My father also started out as a writer, but he always knew that he wanted to be a businessperson. His experience is not the only way people find themselves in business or even come to lead in business. What I've come to see is that business needs creativity as much as the theater does, maybe more at times because its impact is felt so profoundly in our everyday lives. I have been welcomed in today's business climate—a world that now very much wants "accidents" like me.

I was happy when the February 2004 issue of *Harvard Business Review* called the MFA the new MBA. As *HBR* noted, "[A master of fine] arts degree is now perhaps the hottest credential in the world of business. Corporate recruiters have begun visiting the top art grad schools. The supply of people with basic MBA skills is expanding and therefore driving down their value. Meanwhile, the demand for artistic aptitude is surging." (From "Breakthrough Ideas for 2004: The *HBR* List," by Daniel H. Pink.)

New leadership styles—cultivating individuality, dissent, innovation, meritocracy, and unconventional thinking—have never been more important in order for American business to keep hold of its competitive edge. Because of this fact, the productive leadership modalities in business are often different from what they were just ten years ago.

To nourish the indispensable creativity of these new knowledge workers and keep them at their jobs, leaders are going to have to treat them more like craftsmen and artists than like traditional managers; businesses may even consider creating something more akin to a studio environment for them to work in. Management guru Peter Drucker said in a 1996 *Leader to Leader* magazine interview that you have to treat the knowledge workers of today the way you treat volunteers. They are changing the way leadership is practiced.

In an *Atlantic Monthly* article Drucker also says, "Bribery doesn't work anymore" ("Beyond the Information Revolution," October 1999), and he points out that in this culture of knowledge-based workers, where growth and challenge are as important, if not more important, than money, you have to go to lengths to treat people as though they are voluntarily gaining career satisfaction (i.e., doing their job strictly by choice) by being intellectually and emotionally engaged. That is, treat them as visiting dignitaries not wage slaves.

My personal story, and how I "accidentally," thanks to my father, found myself in business, is a tale about me finding out just how much creativity and pragmatism ultimately need each other. The resulting amalgam of those two values touching hands is the source of my (and lots of others) entrepreneurship.

Years ago, the idea of becoming an entrepreneur was nowhere on my radar, but that changed quickly after my son came into the world. My father came down for a visit when my son was just a few months old. I was a social worker (exploring my values) and adjunct university instructor (exploring my creativity) living and working in Asheville, North Carolina. I had never thought about money as a motivator before. I never thought about it because I grew up with my needs met. When I became a father that all changed. I suddenly felt the weight and responsibility my father must have felt but never spoke of—the weight of wanting to provide for your family and how that just automatically comes first. Unless you're a parent, I don't think you can understand that the way I did when I saw my son born.

My son had a terrible case of colic in the beginning, and walking was the only thing that calmed him. So during this visit, I took my dad for a walk on the trails of the arboretum not far from my house. My son was in a baby carrier on my chest and before long he fell asleep there. It was autumn, my favorite time in the mountains, and the yellow, red, and purple blended overhead and around so that after a while we were swimming in color.

I didn't say a word about my worries for the first mile or so of the walk; I was just glad to be out there. I finally spit it out when I couldn't take it anymore: "What about business?" I said to Dad. "I don't want to push Tami to go back to work. Being an adjunct and social worker isn't giving me the time or money to be the father and husband I want to be. . . ." I cut myself off there and told Dad that the bird circling above us was a red-tailed hawk. (I didn't tell him that in Native American mythology the hawk symbolizes a messenger.) Hearing the words come out of my mouth felt too strange to linger on them.

After the air settled back a bit, we talked about options and the idea of me using my skills as a playwright. Dad knew (though I had no idea) there was a whole field of work to write speeches for business leaders and then to coach them on how to address their audience. On the spot, he helped me come up with a plan of action. It is what Dad does best.

And there it was. When we got back to the trailhead, I took my eyes off the near-perfect leaves and looked at Dad. It was like meeting him for the first time, father to father, and without a word, I understood things about him that I never could have before.

Soon after that walk, I moved near New Orleans temporarily, to be close to my in-laws and get some physical support for my young family so I could focus without worry on turning my talent into a viable business. I set up an office in my in-laws' study and, with high-speed Internet access, a borrowed fax machine, and a cell phone, hatched my company, WriteMind Communications. Before long, after a lot of persistence and a bit of luck (those two seem to go together), I was able to return to Asheville with my family and grow my business there. In time, I was able to take my playwriting and directing instincts, coupled with my approach to Zen practice, and turn them into a unique speechwriting and speaker training consultancy that Fortune 500 CEOs were glad to have access to.

A NEW PERSPECTIVE ON CREATIVITY AND LEADERSHIP

I credit that day with my dad in the woods, walking and talking business, as a turning point. He helped me to see an opportunity to use my skills and I took it, and I'm grateful I did, because not only has it allowed me to put my creativity and values into practice on a daily basis, but it has also given me the time and peace of mind to be the father and husband I want to be. With Dad's encouragement, I came to see how indispensable creativity is to business, and business is to creativity. When I entered the business world, it opened up a whole new line of communication between my dad and me. We were now able to talk business and examine the issues we were coming up against and see where we could help each other. I wanted to be a part of this book, so we could show others of differing ages, views, and predilections just how interdependent we all really are.

Additionally, I wanted to do this book because walking was an integral part of the work. I took my cue on this from Thoreau and his simple treatise called *Walking*. Ralph Waldo Emerson said of Thoreau, "The length of his walking made the length of his writing. If shut up in the house, he did not write at all." Thoreau walked at least four hours a day, sometimes more. He felt it essential to remove himself from "worldly engagements" for a part of the day if he was to get any quality thinking and writing done. This has always been true for me. Your mind is freer to roam and think without the ceiling of the office pressing down. There's something about looking up at sky overhead that reminds you that the only limits you impose are your own.

There was something also about being able to chew over these Ps of leadership on a 100-mile journey and reflect on the words of leaders from various disciplines. The more I read about leadership and observe its practice (or lack thereof in various business, academic, and nonprofit environments), the more I come to realize that leadership is the closest thing we have in our economy to applied philosophy. Leadership asks the why questions about work, not just the how and the what. And as I examined each of the leadership practices, I put the why question to each one of them. Most of us know what it means to perform well at work; we also know what it means to persist at work. The question for leadership, though, is why do we do these things?

For a long time many in business believed the simple, transactional idea that we do it for money. But study after study proves that wrong. People work for money only at a very basic level of meeting their needs. Going deeper, researchers have found that people work in order to feel a sense of usefulness, purpose, and identity. And when they cannot feel these things, their performance degrades and they are generally unhappy on the job. At that point, the job is reduced to "a paycheck." Leadership is the practice that, when done with diligence and sincerity, can help to build meaningful contexts for others in which to work. The nine leadership Ps are both descriptive and prescriptive, though bear in mind they are less like a cave to explore and more like a tunnel to go through and emerge from. The light to search out on the other side is your own.

CHAPTER 1

PEOPLE

When Ideas Lead, People Follow

Focus on people and the numbers will come. Focus on numbers and the people will go.—WILLIAM TOPPETA, PRESIDENT, METLIFE INTERNATIONAL

I think the day that your people stop bringing their problems to you
is the day you stop leading. They've either concluded that you
don't care about their problems or that you cannot help them.
And leaders have to be in a position to help.
—JEFF RICH, CEO OF AFFILIATED COMPUTER SERVICES, INC. (ACS)

It was our first morning in New Orleans and Jonathon and I spent it having breakfast at a place called "Mother's." Fried eggs, biscuits, gravy, sausage, grits—forget about the Atkins Diet in New Orleans. And besides the great food, the southern charm of "Hey, sweetie" was a nice change from the typical greeting of "What da ya want?" at a New York City luncheonette. We both liked the idea of a father and son starting the day at a place called "Mother's." After all, it's where the vast majority of us first get started. Our first leader, if you will, is mother.

One of the things that made us laugh hysterically that morning is that I showed up at breakfast in a gray T-shirt and shorts and Jon showed up in a button-down polo shirt and dress slacks (brand-me-downs I had sent him.) I didn't want to clash with his laid-back style and he didn't want to overly contrast with my businesslike demeanor. We dressed as the other prefers for the sake of making the other feel comfortable. After we got through laughing at ourselves, we realized that something was going on: We were showing sensitivity about who we each were. Sometimes to acknowledge and show you have respect for somebody else, you need to downplay your persona and get into theirs . . . and to laugh about it! When you see beyond appearances and labels, you get a chance to speak right to the heart of a person. How many of us take the time to do that with our colleagues at work? Life would be so different if we did.

After breakfast we walked through New Orleans, this French, Spanish, and American cultural amalgamation with street names and architecture that make you feel as though you're walking through a tiny part of Europe. When we got to Jackson Square, we stopped to look at what the crowd was staring at. Upon closer inspection, we realized what they were looking at was a woman painted silver from head to toe, standing frozen solid on top of a silver milk crate. Whenever someone put a dollar in the silver box in front of her, she would play her snare drum for a minute. "Now, there's a possible leader," Jonathon said to me. I smiled at the joke. "I'm serious," he said. Yes, she had followers; yes, she was taking a risk. But to my mind, she was a spectacle, not a leader.

Jonathon said she was getting people to stop their usual routine and "pay attention." To him, there was something essential about this activity. I didn't see at the time what he meant, but I let it go. We soon walked on, exploring more of the city, venturing deeper into its sordid history and its eclectic present.

Among the people I would call true leaders—those I have interviewed, those who have come to speak at the Fordham Leadership Forum, those with whom I have worked, and those I read about—there is consensus that when it comes to people, you need to recruit, develop, and reward people who are as smart or smarter than

> ## *Jon:*
>
> *To spot a leader I don't look for titles, I look for actions—actions compelling enough to bring others into the center of the present moment. For a leader to do her job, first and foremost, she must be certain that those around her are awake and on the same page.*

you are. And I would add that you have to accept their pushback and have the courage to push back at them in order to help them be more than they imagined they ever could be.

It is the people, not the products, of an organization that can make a mediocre vision soar or sabotage an outstanding one. A leader can never forget this fact and does all she can to continually learn what her people need to do their best work. To hire people at least as smart as you (or hopefully smarter) in areas in which you do not excel, you have to be comfortable with your own self-esteem and appreciative of your own unique gifts. If you have trouble appreciating who you are, work on it. Because if you don't, you'll spend a lifetime needing the approval of others, and leaders don't have time for that. Having insecurities that affect your work, and not being aware of them, is the death of someone in a leader's role. When you're out front in your organization, the more you don't recognize, acknowledge, and work with your insecurities and faults, the more obvious they become to the people you are supposed to be leading. If you don't like the idea of surrounding yourself with ambitious, passionate, bright, and self-motivated achievers, you have to ask yourself why not and deal with that. People who expect the best of their own work and are willing to challenge you will ultimately make you look good. "Yes people" do not. They may make you feel good briefly, but in the long run, they will take you down and shatter an organization.

BE THE LEADER

Hire people you personally would follow.

To lead people, you don't have to be the IQ leader of the pack. Be the best motivator, the best listener, the best facilitator, and the best identifier of best ideas, and by all means, hire people who know tons of stuff you haven't even imagined. Most of all, keep your ego in check. The practice and craft of leading people is about taking on the great individual talents and skills in your sector and fitting them into a montage where every person has her specialized domain.

I'll give you an example that changed the way I hire people. When I took over at my advertising agency, then called Robert A. Becker, there was a bookkeeper who had been with the company for fifteen years. She was a high school grad with no formal education in financial dealings, but she was known to be a whiz with numbers. As assistant to the then CFO, this bookkeeper, Terry Wachalter, taught me the financial inner workings of our organization through her clear and cogent explanations. I wound up firing three high-priced CFOs, all of whom couldn't seem to improve the reporting of the financials or explain company goals to me in simple financial terms, not to mention match Wachalter's zeal for our company's mission.

Though she refused the post at first, eventually Wachalter became our CFO. Not one to let herself off the hook, she assessed where she personally had to grow and enrolled in public speaking and business management classes. She became a knowledge "sponge," given all the books she read about running an organization. As you might expect, she was promoted to chief of operations not long after, and she ran the tightest ship around for the many years we worked together. She had everyone's respect because she earned it with her performance and demeanor, not with her résumé credentials.

As a leader you have to surround yourself with people who want to grow and welcome being pushed to become better tomorrow than they were yesterday. One of the slogans the Marine Corps is known for is "Grow or go," and I couldn't agree more. Find the best and push them to be better—and when they push back and ask the same of you, smile to yourself, because you've done your job.

Jeff Rich, CEO of ACS, puts it about as succinctly as you can: "Every leader worth a damn will tell you that their success is the result of the smart, talented people working with them. And I'm no different." Real leaders have a good opinion of themselves. They don't need glory; but what they do need is confidence, great advice, great support, and great help (some recognition at appropriate times helps, too). The weak ones—and we've all witnessed one or two firsthand—characterize any kind of pushback as disloyalty and, as a result, tend to surround themselves with weak "yes" people.

The first time I heard this idea of hiring people smarter than you was from Tom Peters in his 1982 watershed book, *In Search of Excellence*. Peters is still weighing in on the subject twenty-five years later, and the degree to which he was right just grows from year to year. There was a time fifty years ago or more, in some businesses even twenty years ago, when one or two people knew all there was to know about a given subject, technology, or product. Today, such an achievement is simply impossible. A hundred years ago the

Wright Brothers knew all there was to know about flying and they were able to get off the ground on account of their own know-how. But as technology progresses, there is almost no way a situation like that can remain. For a plane to be airborne today, you need exacting specialists not only in flight, but also in computer programming, electronics, air traffic, aerodynamics, and many other specialties that need to come together.

The nature of business today parallels this interdisciplinary complexity. A multitude of skills and strengths need to weave together to create, market, and sell a single idea or product. The concept that the leader of an organization can know everything expertly is a fallacy, but the one expert skill she can never do without is recognizing smart and motivated people and giving them the autonomy to do their jobs in their sector, and then rewarding them accordingly.

When the president of MetLife's international business, Bill Toppeta, spoke to my students about the necessity of developing people skills, he summed it up this way: "More leaders fail for lack of people skills than fail for lack of technical skills. The technical skills are the price of admission. When you graduate, you'll have your MBA. You'll have your ticket punched and most employers will not question the fact that you have technical skills. These technical skills are the price of entry, but it is the people skills that will allow you to rise in the company's leadership."

Regarding that other kind of manager, the one not interested in letting others into the spotlight, the dynamic Jeff Rich gave the class this image to chew on. "I call them shade trees," he said, "because they're huge; they soak up all the sunshine coming down on their organization, and they don't let any of the credit go below them." And relying just on financial compensation to grow loyalty isn't enough, people need to be recognized in other ways.

This presumption is so different from the world I came up in.

Leading today means you need to acknowledge that talented people have lots of other options. If you want them to work productively for you, your work environment has to be a place in which they can take real ownership.

An interesting example of a young leader practicing this skill is thirty-seven-year-old Jeffrey Aronin, the energetic CEO of Chicago-based Ovation Pharmaceuticals, Inc. Under his leadership, the company raised $150 million for its pharmaceutical pursuits. I've known Aronin for a while and respect him and his leadership style. Recently I accepted a position on his company's advisory board. Both Jonathon and I have talked to him and interviewed him extensively about his leadership practices. Aronin is around the same age as my son Jon, but the nature of their career paths couldn't be more different. Though I'm a few decades older than him, I have a whole lot more in common with him than Jon does. It's not always age, but often personality and style that bring difference to the workplace. Stereotypes of any sort don't help us. In fact, they can muddle your perception and ability to get things done.

Here is Jeff Aronin's story. In his early career, he was a sales representative with Carter-Wallace, a Fortune 500 pharmaceutical company. It should come as no surprise that he was rated one of the top reps every year. A division manager by the time he was twenty-four, he became the youngest division director in Carter-Wallace history. Then, fortuitously, a retiring top executive who had just purchased a division of a well-known competitive drug manufacturer, now renamed AHP or American Health Products, approached him. He proposed that Aronin come aboard and run the company with him and then succeed him. It was a risky proposition, but Jeff Aronin accepted and managed to triple the sales at the new company. Following that feat, he was just getting ready for a new adventure when it was announced that the company had been sold. The venture had done very well and the same venture capitalists who had backed AHP wanted to back Aronin again, this time as CEO of his own company. He took them up on this new exciting challenge and ended up taking this next company, Med-Care, public. After one more successful start-up transformation and strategic sale through his leadership of RxMarketing, Aronin was finally ready in 2000 to take on his current venture, Ovation Pharmaceuticals, where he acquires and develops specialty drugs for smaller patient populations. Ovation led one of the biggest public financings in 2001, and the company is well on its way to forging a great future for its investors.

Aronin told me that the greatest gift his partners ever gave him was the freedom to fail. Although failure was never coddled or excused, it was analyzed and learned from. He said this fact energized and pushed him to work his way through failure toward success. "You have to continually bet on yourself to build confidence," he says. Emulating what his mentors did for him, Aronin describes himself as a manager whose key role is to be there to advise and direct, not to control. He says if he completely controls his people, they will never understand the necessity to "bet on themselves." He credits many of his leadership skills to his practice of hiring people smarter and more experienced than he is. "I hire people to be part of my executive committee who have proven themselves in the industry to be some of the smartest and wisest people around. I watch them and study their behavior in crisis and in the day to day. I always had a knack for being an entrepreneur," Aronin adds, "but I work on becoming a leader through watching other leaders, like my advisory committee members. Learning happens every minute and eventually you absorb it and integrate it into your practice."

Jeff Aronin is a great example of a young emerging leader who is secure enough with his own abilities to go out and hire the absolute best he can find. Of course, it doesn't hurt my feelings that these best/smarter people tend to be older, seasoned leaders who have done it before and proved themselves. There are loads of other companies out there, though, that are in need of other kinds of skills. A large multimedia conglomerate, for example, may require the best people in gaming technology. And sometimes the best is a nineteen-year-old college dropout who can write amazing code, but getting him to wear a business suit to a staff meeting is an absurdity. Obviously, this situation wouldn't make me feel as comfortable, but it is reality, and if we are not open to it we fail.

BE THE DIRECTOR OF EDUCATION

Teach your people all the time and encourage others to do the same.

Employee training and development is not an episodic event, it's an ongoing daily process. Leaders can't only be great doers, they also have to be great teachers, and that's a time-consuming effort. Remember the old adage, "Those that can't do, teach." Well, forget about it if you want to lead. To be an effective leader of people, you have to do both every day . . . continually.

There is always that condescending manager who says, "I can't be bothered with training, I have too much of my own work to do." I say look out—that's a manager who will be quick to blame the new hire for not knowing the ropes at the big client meeting. Really, whose fault is it? It's the fault of the manager (note how I did not say leader) who mistakenly believes that tending to her "to do" list is more important than training her greatest assets—her people. And, sad to say, a lot of middle managers, senior people, and even entrepreneurs don't grasp this truth. They expect their people to come fully formed and trained. It never works out that way. One of the most successful of entrepreneurs in the last twenty years, Howard Schultz of Starbucks Corp., is living proof that it's in the training that the mission is set and the vision is clarified to the benefit of the company. In my experience, I have not met any young leader who does this as passionately and consistently as Myrtle Potter, Genentech, Inc.'s COO. As a speaker at the Fordham Leadership Forum, Potter said:

> "I'm not here in my role because I am gifted or bright; I am here because I learned very early on [that] the number-one job we have as leaders is to ensure that we've got capable people working with us who are emotionally committed, can buy into a vision, and who are willing and ready to give it their all. And once you are certain that you have that, your number-one responsibility is to help these people grow, develop, and exceed all of their personal goals as they take their careers to the next level."

In 2002, *Time* magazine named Myrtle Potter one of the top fifteen "Young Global Business Influentials," and *Fortune* ranked her number eighteen on its list of the "Most Powerful Black Executives in America." But none of that is what it is about for Potter. She wouldn't discuss that stuff with the class. What she wanted to do was talk about a leader's responsibility:

> "You get accolades, you get recognition, you get all the wonderful things that come with it, but at the end of the day, if you're not teaching people what you know, what good are you as a leader? There's only one of me. If I'm not multiplying my impact by putting my knowledge and insights in the hands of others, then I'm cheating myself and the business. The number-one obligation a leader has is to put other people in a position to lead on their own."

Education Rarely Happens in the Classroom—It Happens One-on-One with a Mentor

Mentoring people to grow into the leaders they are capable of becoming is far from a cut-and-dried process. In the best cases, mentorship is never a one-way street. It requires a bit of finesse to encourage someone not of your generation to grow. The balance between irritating and enticing is a thin line. An element that can be very beneficial between mentor and mentee is the one Jonathon and I are trying to practice in our work on this book together— *reverse mentorship*. It is also a practice that I instituted at Becker. (How else would I have learned to download music, keep up with *Survivor*, and program my BlackBerry?) I hope my two young mentors learned as much from me as I did from them. We learn more when we listen than when we talk (dare I remind you of the cliché about having two ears and one mouth?), and having a mentor in reverse is an important way to learn what motivates and inspires young and new hires in your company.

Randy Thurman, CEO and chairman of VIASYS Healthcare, Inc., talked to us about the results of a leadership study he participated in through the University of Pennsylvania a few years back. In that study, they discovered that almost all successful leaders had both overcome a great adversity in their lives and had at least one great mentor. For women in the study, having a great mentor was the number-one factor they cited as a key to their success as leaders.

When you are leading an organization, it is easy to forget sometimes that people are not problems to be fixed, like items on a business plan. People are complex, diverse, and require special attention. When it comes to people, the work is not about "getting it done." People are not something "to do," but rather people are a collection of experiences to understand, and from those experiences they grow.

When an employee looks at a leader, he should see himself reflected—a story both of what he is and what he can be. I think it is within the very act of leading that the leader is transformed. When leaders are in sync with their followers, both are transformed by the experience of having a focused mission and overcoming difficult obstacles together.

Teach with Stories and Unplanned Moments

Whether you're two or eighty-two, people love the tales of their own and other people's triumphs—it helps to shape the legend of the workplace. Leaders have to be storytellers in their formal talks to staff members because their people learn, process new information, and maintain memories in story form. Storytelling also provides an ethos in the workplace that establishes the key norms of your company's people culture. Is your company one where leadership positions are given to those who earn them through merit, or because of the seniority they've accumulated or connections they've made? Every story tells a story.

Just like individuals, companies need positive folklore that enforces a positive culture. Positive messages have to be communicated on a large scale, and people need to be inspired to overcome pettiness. Peter Drucker's claim that the only three things that come naturally to an organization are "friction, confusion, and underperformance" is all too accurate. What CEO doesn't wear the hat of chief psychiatrist when managing so many diverse needs and personalities? To get something positive out of your people, you have to work at it skillfully and creatively every day. It's difficult but satisfying work.

You need to demonstrate that you practice what you preach. Leaders need to model the message all the time. Former New York City fire commissioner and 9/11 hero Thomas Von Essen told the students at Fordham how he models his message of leadership. Alluding to all the high-priced fund-raisers he found himself attending after 9/11, he said: "I'm a person who is a lot nicer to the busboy than I am to the maître d'. That's just me . . . I relate to the person at the bottom. And I appreciate what they do. When I see somebody treating people who are less fortunate than they are disrespectfully, or without any recognition, I lose all respect for that person."

What matters to Von Essen is that his people know they are valued. If you berate the busboy but fawn over the maître d', then what kind of a message does that send to your employees on the front lines of your operation? Nothing speaks louder to your people than a moment caught "off the record."

According to Bill Shore, founder and executive director of the nonprofit Share Our Strength and a former political consultant, the key moment in any political campaign often comes when the true identity of the candidate is revealed as a result of some unplanned, inadvertent action. At that point all the creative spin in the world cannot rescue a candidate from his own actions. From my own experience, I can say this is positively true all the time—the microphone remains on even when you think you're off camera. And at those moments, more than at the scripted ones, your people are really paying attention and learning what you are all about. Don't underestimate the significance placed on the leader's public persona at the workplace. Even when you don't think you're teaching your employees something about yourself, the company culture, or what you think of your colleagues, they inevitably are learning.

BE A MOTIVATOR . . . THROUGH MORE HARD WORK

Work hard to get the best out of your people.

Help your people to identify what their strengths are and give them the opportunity to use them. Spending an inordinate amount of time working on your people's weaknesses, as most training managers do, is time wasted. Focus on their strengths. Great leaders are interested in helping future leaders step up and lead. Greg Young, former CEO of CorePharma Holdings, Inc., a leading developer and manufacturer of solid dose generic pharmaceuticals, told me a story that underscores this point. In his early thirties, Young worked for a Fortune 500 company called G.D. Searle & Company (now part of Pfizer). He was in marketing and his boss gave him a tremendous opportunity to put together a team of people who would be charged with creating a new, innovative launch for a product. Problem was, Young had no authority over his colleagues. He reminded his boss that he didn't have any people directly reporting to him. "I know," his boss said. "Go get people excited and sell them on this thing—let your ideas speak for you and see who wants to join."

According to Young, that experience taught him the essence of leadership—that people follow you not because of your rank, but because of your ideas, enthusiasm, and credibility, and because they sense you would be willing to give credit to others for a job well done. More evidence that Peter Drucker was right about the importance of enlisting volunteers to your cause, and about being wary of relying on hierarchical structures to determine who leads.

I've known Greg Young for more than twenty years. Hierarchy still doesn't mean a whole lot to him. Those lessons at Searle served him well. When Jon interviewed him after he gave his talk at Fordham, Young told Jon about another earlier job experience. It was after Searle, at Baxter Healthcare Corporation, where he had someone reporting to him who in turn had six people reporting to him. Young didn't lay eyes on those other six people for a year, so he began to wonder if his direct report had locked them up somewhere. At every presentation given by his group, this manager was always the one doing the presenting solo. Even if Young would ask to hear from the people who helped with the work, his direct report was adamant about handling it all himself and keeping his people away. I cite this example because Young fired this guy. Not because he couldn't do great work and get a lot out of people, which he could, but because he was unable to allow his people to grow and advance.

Seconding Drucker in his own way, Bill Gray, the president of Ogilvy & Mather New York, part of the top-ten global advertising organization, told the MBAs that in his opinion the biggest recurring mistake a leader makes is not realizing that you can't be smart about everything and that you need people who know things you don't. Know you'll have uncertainty every day, he told the class. Given today's business volatility, you need to cultivate trust and plainspokenness to overcome fears within your organization.

Because people are beings with emotions, dreams, worries, and needs, you can't "manage" them as though they are quantifiable resources. Forget about the moral implications, such treatment simply won't work in the long term. This seems pretty obvious; yet in business, where we deal with a crisis a day, we forget sometimes. People like Bill Toppeta of MetLife are human reminders of how such behavior is actually negative for a company's bottom line. Toppeta is hands-down one of the best communicators I've ever met. He spends 60 percent of his time on the road conversing with and talking to MetLife's 47,000 employees worldwide. To him, a leader's job is to provide a mind-set, a space where people can grow to their full potential. He says he travels that much not because he wants to inspire MetLife's people, but because he wants to show them how they can inspire themselves.

I have to confess that I wasn't sure I had a solid grasp on what Toppeta meant by teaching others to inspire themselves until I watched the Olympics and the men's individual all-around gymnastics competition in August 2004. I watched Paul Hamm, the twenty-one-year-old American and favorite to win the competition, fall right on his backside and into the judges' box as he landed from his high flying vault. Any reasonable person would have known it was over—four years down the drain. That's what all the sportscasters were saying. They called it a "devastating tragedy," a horrific moment Paul Hamm would remember for the rest of his life. Said the commentators, there was no way he could concentrate on the next two events in front of him: the parallel bars and the high bar. He would be too busy kicking himself mentally. But were they wrong! Paul Hamm put forth the performance of his life on the next two events and came back from twelfth place to win the gold medal. The commentators turned out to be right about one thing, Hamm would never forget that fall he took. But not for the reasons they assumed. Hamm would remember it as a mark of how he was able to inspire and motivate himself to win. When interviewed he said simply, "I just remembered what my coach had always told me—the meet is not over until it's over."

When I watched that performance I thought not only of this young man's character, but of the character of his coach, who could do nothing for him during the performance, save watch. He couldn't execute for him or inspire him in the moment. Something deeper had to be going on for success to happen—Paul Hamm drew inspiration from his gut. Whatever the seed of motivation and drive the coach planted had to have taken root a long time before this single performance. His coach is a leader, not because of what he did for Hamm, but because of what he long ago taught him—to be able to do it for himself.

I'm thinking about how Myrtle Potter got her start. At the beginning of her career, she spent fourteen years at Merck & Co. in a variety of key sales, marketing, and business planning roles. She was one of the architects of the Astra/Merck joint venture that set Prilosec, the acid reflux drug, on pace to be a worldwide blockbuster. Although Potter accomplished all of this before turning forty, it did not start out easy for her. When she was promoted to her first senior management role at Merck she was excited about her brand-new job. She thought she had a capable team of people to help her execute the goals she had been entrusted with; but when she began working with them, most of the team was resistant to working with her to define a new vision. It was all circular dialogues in meetings, and she felt a palpable pushback from her people.

Fortunately for her, it was right about then that she was selected to attend leadership guru Noel Tichy's six-week leadership training program for global executives. Tichy personally pressed Potter about her people and their lack of positive response to her. Naturally, as we all do at first, she wanted to explain it away. She told Tichy she hoped her group would get over her being so much younger and getting the job that they believed they "deserved." She said that the whole thing would just take time. She also told Tichy that the business she was now assigned had ranked dead last at Merck and she had been hired to turn the unit around. After three weeks working with Potter on her skills, Tichy thought she was finally ready to hear the truth. "You run a $1 billion business," he said, "it is dead last, it's going down the toilet. And my news to you is something's got to happen between now and the end of the year. Either your folks are not going to be there or you're not going to be there. What's it going to be?" Tichy looked right at her and stated the situation simply: "This is real, and this is not play. What are you going to do to fix the business?"

And that was Potter's wake-up call. She spent the next three weeks of the leadership training program analyzing how to restructure her business unit so it could get back on track and move forward. When she got back to her job, she replaced all but two people on her management team, brought in new staff willing to work together to develop a vision, and lo and behold, the business quickly turned around. Her lesson: realizing there is no future in trying to ride a dead horse. If, as a leader, you think it is *always* your job to get people inspired, you'll burn out quick. People have to want to inspire themselves, and you are only the catalyst . . . not the cause. You have to trust that people have it in them to inspire themselves, and good managers will get out of their people's way and let them do it. If they show you that they don't have the stuff, then you have to cut them loose. As a leader, you have to recognize the limits of your powers. You may be able to bring out greatness that is already within others, but you cannot create something that doesn't already exist. Play to their strengths, not their weaknesses.

HAVE THE COURAGE TO TELL IT STRAIGHT

Reward great performers and be direct
and honest with underachievers.

Our Fordham leaders tell us that great people are how a company ultimately thrives in a sluggish economy. In a great economy, lots of mediocre people fly high and just glom on to the momentum. But when times are tough, it's the self-motivated achievers who make companies not only survive but go beyond expectations. It blows my mind when I hear the dictum, "No bonuses, and no increases, across the board." Although I've been in those situations—dictated to me by the parent company—I've always found a way to get around the problem and reward my top performers.

Bill Toppeta has said, "It's hard to be liked when you're the one telling an employee that his performance is not up to snuff. But my experience is that if you are honest with people, ultimately they will respond in one of two ways: Either they'll respect you for it and work harder, or they'll leave . . . and in either case that's not so bad." Consensus among the Fordham leaders was that to be effective you have to be respected and admired, not necessarily liked.

When Howard Safir was commissioner of the New York City Police Department, he did something daring when it came to selecting his first deputy commissioner, his number-two person. Safir is a strong advocate for the necessity of going against the ingrained culture of an organization when he thinks it will help the organization renew itself. The role of the first deputy commissioner is to take over the job of commissioner if he should become incapacitated for any reason. The position requires that the person be able to do the job as well as the commissioner without interruption or compromise. Safir interviewed all the chiefs in rank order from the four stars to the one stars. The person he finally wound up picking to serve as his first deputy commissioner was a one-star chief. Safir picked him over all the four stars because he believed in the individual's honor, record, and sense of duty to the job.

This choice produced a lot of fallout in the organization. Safir put merit above bureaucratic procedure and threw a wrench in the way of civil service. The other chiefs were angry that this upstart one-star chief was going to be their boss. But Safir believed that just as the man had won him over with his character and quality, so too would he win over the others. And not because of his rank, but because of who he was and what he was capable of doing. "Quality is beyond rank," Safir told me. And his courage as a leader proved out once again. The other New York City deputies came to deeply respect the first deputy commissioner and Safir, for having had the guts to do what he thought was right when he knew full well the decision would not be popular and plenty of officers would be cursing him for it. A decision like that can change an entire culture of an organization. It can take a sleepy organization and rouse it.

Do all managers give more weight to merit than seniority? I wish I could say yes! It's more the exception than the rule in traditional organizations. But that is changing. In this rapidly moving world, wise leaders realize that the people to recruit are the ones who come with an urgency to grow without limits.

One of my favorite maxims from the daring Herb Kelleher, chairman of Southwest Airlines, is "Hire for attitude, train for skill." I must say it to the HR people at least twice a month. Big difficulties can arise when you hire people who have great skills "on paper" and they turn out to have a terrible attitude. Skills can be learned, but a bad attitude is a personal problem, and if that person can't find it within herself to get with the program, she has to be fired.

And by the way, anybody who says "I've fired a lot of people and it's become part of the drill for me" is either psychotic or a liar. I still get sick the night before I have to fire anybody. But when employees fall short, you have to have the courage to walk your talk, to confront the issue and make the change. It's difficult to terminate an associate, be it someone new or someone you've worked with forever, but you have to do what you have to do. I don't know anyone really good at it. But if you can't do it, you risk losing the respect of your top performers. They'll look elsewhere for a level playing field. Bill Toppeta makes the point that it's best to show respect for the person even when you have to strongly criticize performance. This can be a real challenge, but as the wise chair of the Leader to Leader Institute and former head of the Girl Scouts of America, Frances Hesselbein, once told me, sometimes good leadership just comes down to good manners.

Staffers who step up to bat and make it happen every day deserve recognition and compensation for their efforts, regardless of whether the company is in good or bad economic times. Just as you have to have the courage to take out your weak players, you must take care of your great achievers no matter what, because if you don't, they'll walk.

Leading is as much about letting go of your people as it is about holding on to them. What I mean here is giving your employees space into which they can personally excel. If they're that good, you need to make them feel that they are accomplishing big objectives, stretching the envelope. In the long term, if you don't provide your self-motivated achievers a chance to really prove themselves, they won't respect your vision and undoubtedly they'll move on.

TRUST YOUR GUT INSTINCTS

Learn what your people value.

I'll never forget how nervous I was the first time I met John Glenn. I had met his wife, Annie, a stutterer like me, while attending the Hollins Communications Research Institute in Virginia, where we would go the second weekend in July for a refresher course on speech therapy. This particular year, Annie had arranged a lunch for us just before John went back up in space. I was always a huge admirer, and I prepared a list of questions I wanted to ask him.

"What does it feel like to look back at the earth and see it as a sphere? How do you think you'll see earth now compared to forty years ago?" and on and on and on. But before I could even begin with the barrage, Glenn started the conversation (I think to put me at ease). He said, "Sander, what I'd really like is to learn more about you. Annie talks about you all the time. What's your story?"

Just like that, John Glenn opened up the door to inclusion and social equality, and I saw how he led by embracing people to his purpose, including yours truly. The sense you got about him was that he was receptive—that you could tell him anything. Lots of people have medals and titles; but to be a leader, not just a hero, you have to have that desire and instinct to listen to others and be genuinely interested in what you hear. If you can't do that, you're going to have a real problem sustaining a leadership role.

Karen Dawes has been a corporate veteran for more than twenty years. She's held some of the biggest jobs in the pharmaceutical industry, including senior vice president, division head, Bayer Pharmaceuticals corporation in the United States. In 2003, Dawes founded Knowledgeable Decisions, LLC, a consulting firm that focuses on assisting emerging pharmaceutical companies in commercialization. She explained her decision to go out on her own in this way:

> "On 9/11, I was actually in the air flying to a sales meeting and was diverted to Savannah, Georgia, where I spent twenty-four hours alone waiting for a colleague to come pick me up so we could drive back up the East Coast. In that time I did a lot of thinking. One of the things that I said to myself was that, if within a year I could not wake up and say I absolutely love my life, I was going to change it. During that year I began to look, really look, at my life. I was traveling overseas a few times a month, working long hours. I would get up at 6 A.M. Saturday

morning and do two hours of e-mails. I basically said I just don't want to do this anymore. It was the hardest decision I ever made . . . and I have no regrets."

For people like Karen Dawes to remain in big corporations, organizations will have to focus on actively being responsive to employees of talent and creating incentives of meaning.

I learned from futurist Faith Popcorn, frequent speaker at the Fordham Leadership Forum, and my marketing consultant wife, Mechele, that much of the impetus for companies to create incentives of meaning has to do with the growing percentage of women in high-powered jobs in corporate America. Women have knowingly and unknowingly reshaped some of the very basics of what we perceive as great leadership. Because so many women are in the workplace, more organizations allot effort and resources and develop practices to keep employees, male and female, personally happy. Women are at the center of this trend, both as employers and employees.

It was the unwritten code for men in the past not to talk about their families at work, but when women came into corporate America in significant numbers, they would not stand for that kind of compartmentalization of life. It's crazy when you start thinking that work was once a place where people felt they had to hide something as human as their own family life. Today, we are just starting to open up to this reality, to give proper recognition to the concept that "working" includes the full life of your workers and not just the result of the work-product they produce for you. We still have a long way to go before the workplace is instead thought of as the "people place." Women and many other groups not part of the traditional "old (white) guy" network have helped us start to get there. It's heartening that at least some organizations have begun to demonstrate that they value what their employees value. And the result is that when employees see this trend they work harder.

Jonathon's Perspective

People love as self-recognition what
they hate as accusation.
—Elias Canetti

When you walk through the woods you notice what is out of the ordinary. After a few miles, the green, brown, and gray almost disappear into nothing and what you feel is simply rhythm, pace, and continuity of environment. A birdcall can break the relative peace and calm, or the hammering of a woodpecker into a tulip poplar, or a solitary red leaf in September that decided to change from green earlier than the rest. Other than that, you don't particularly notice your environment as much as absorb it. In a way, the same can be said about a crowded city. The uproar of Bourbon Street, the tarot card readers of Jackson Square, the waiters of near-empty restaurants posted outside their doorways trying to entice you inside with a menu in hand—you can walk by them all in New Orleans because they begin to blend into one large landscape that can be absorbed without having to be personally experienced.

But for some reason, a woman painted silver, standing on a silver box, with a silver snare drum clasped to her waist, demands to be experienced. She is playing on our sense of expectation the same way a red leaf does in September. It is not supposed to be that way. Someone standing as still as she has managed should be a stone statue, not a fleshy person with pumping blood.

Her presence expressed an imperative aspect of leadership to me. Without a word, she was asking people to pay attention to their environment. Her posture afforded her the ability to play with people's expectations of reality. If statues are made to look like people, why can't people be made to look like statues? Such a playful question got many travelers to stop in a city that offers a lot of competing spectacles. Regarding leadership, her actions, to me, are emblematic of how you get the best out of people—you must gently disrupt them into paying attention to you. If staffers are not paying attention to the leader and her vision, then the future becomes cloudy. This means leaders have to focus on doing something counterintuitive, something that people cannot simply absorb as part and parcel of the landscape, but something instead that forces them to come to terms with the very moment transpiring in front of them.

The silver woman defied expectations of how human bodies generally behave. And that picture is what intrigued people and got them to stop and notice. Effective leaders, whom I've interviewed and observed in action, do not didactically ask their followers to pay attention; they playfully beckon them to arrive at the sort of attention through which creative work can best be accomplished.

A demand feels like an insult because it implies a lack of trust. If the silver lady were demanding something of us, we wouldn't feel as comfortable to stop and pay attention and engage. Demands imply hierarchy: "I have power, and you don't, so listen to me and execute the goals I want you to execute." On the other hand, if a leader presents an issue from a horizontal standpoint—"We are facing challenge A, I have B thoughts about it; what steps do you think might bring us closer to a solution?"—this exchange is an invitation to engage a shared issue that, if solved, will benefit the entire company.

Howard Safir's story of how he hired his first deputy commissioner has particular resonance for me in that he took merit over seniority. He did the unexpected and woke up a culture. With his action, Safir invited his people to see themselves as individually valued, not bureaucratic entities that pass tests, get stars, and get promoted without question. Safir invited human relations to take precedence over procedure and tradition. Such a move sends a resounding message to people in my generation; that such a thing could happen at the New York City Police Department at the highest level makes a noticeable impact.

Karen Dawes's story also brings up a point worth going over. When it comes to 9/11 having been a watershed event, I think you can multiply her story by the tens of thousands. That day was a call for people to take stock of what is most meaningful to them. Dawes's big epiphany was that she chose to step away from corporate life and found her own company. Her 9/11 experience helped her to recognize that she wanted to be more independent, to have a more flexible life, and to try being her own boss—in short, to have a life. To go after this dream, she had to change her working lifestyle. She and many other baby boomer comrades want to have more, and events such as 9/11 reinforce that desire.

For me and quite a number in my generation, time is not money; time is time. I know that if I spend it all at work rather than with my child, spouse, family, and friends, or on my own personal well-being, then I have lost it forever. Money, promotions, cars, and big houses do not buy you back time, nor do they provide you with needed peace of mind. I always knew this, and suspect lots of my friends did, too. Maybe it's because we watched the boomer generation tell itself "You can have it all," and then come to the sad realization that such a thing was impossible. I think I learned a lot from my parents' struggles with trying to balance home and work. I also learned from James Chung, principal of Reach Advisors in Boston, who conducted a study featured in *Fortune* in which he polled 3,000 Gen Xers. As he explained to me, for Generation X, it is not about fitting family life into work (as it was for the boomers in large numbers); rather, it is about fitting work into family life. What does that say for the practice of leadership when it comes to managing my generation?

I think it means that people have to be permitted to bring their full selves to the office and be made to feel as though their lives come first. People cannot be asked to put on a "show" where they pretend that the late-day meeting is more important than giving their young child a bath and putting her to bed. This doesn't mean people are "soft" or want to work less. It means they want to work smarter, more flexibly, efficiently, and without ever having to make a choice between professional and personal priorities; they want to work where it is openly acknowledged that the personal always comes first. Creative leadership can bring out the best in this situation by making work a place of meaning for people—one that provides personal and occupational satisfaction, where the personal is not shut off, as it was in the past, but where it is let in and built upon.

The key for the leader, I think, is not to oppose, but to try and integrate—for the leader to see that employees value their lives as family members, parents, and friends and also deeply want to be loyal and dedicated employees. One does not exclude the other. As long as the order of importance of the values stays uncompromised, there will be great productivity at work and the potential for real happiness. Tamper with that order for long, and you invite resentment, unhappiness, and burnout (and don't rule out new employment searches).

I want to say a bit about stories and their importance. I'm with Dad on this point. As human beings, we want to make meaning out of our lives. Stories help us to put our lives into a meaning-rich context. A leader is more than the acts she commits in the daily rounds of her job. The leader holds a place of mythic importance when it comes to the company story. But before your thoughts go to the "Great Oz" presenting the company story from some implacable perch, forget it. Everyone needs to be a part of this story. Leaders need to set up an open-ended text, one poised for interruption and insertion of other narratives. Rather than the melting-pot model of every person fitting into the monolithic company story, tomorrow's leaders will be asked to make room for the myth to shift, to change and grow according to the makeup of the actual people working at the company and invested in its success. That the company is the people is the story.

And how does a story or myth take shape? It is made real when it is publicly told. Imagine how different Homer's *Iliad* would be if you had heard it recounted over a fire pit each night for a period of weeks with friends, as the ancient Greeks did, compared to reading it silently on your own in a freshman dorm? It is the same for a company story: It has to be enacted, retold, added to, and encouraged. A good story shows us the meaning of our lives. A good company story shows us the meaning of our work lives. The telling of stories about genuine people, and how they made the company what it is, is a powerful experience. Spare me and all your employees if you think you can do this manipulatively through the internal corporate communications department. Gen Xers would never take that seriously. And corporate storytelling cannot be a one-time event. Companies change, people change, and to remain meaningful, the stories must make room, remain open, and adapt to the new circumstances and find richness therein.

Finally, I believe that a great leader is willing to step up for his people. I saw this pointedly in another summer 2004 Olympics story, this one about nineteen-year-old swimmer Michael Phelps.

A day before Phelps and his U.S.A. teammates were about to swim the Olympic relay, he decided to give up his spot to teammate Ian Crocker, who had yet to receive a medal in the Games. In so doing, Phelps certainly inspired Crocker to inspire himself, and beyond that he inspired the entire team. With five gold medals and two bronzes already in hand, Phelps could afford to be generous; many still aren't. But he was, and he cheered Crocker harder than anyone in the stands. His team broke the world record and Phelps got his sixth gold (because he swam in the relay prelim), but to get that gold he had to let go of the outcome and trust that his teammates would bring it home for him. Ultimately, his leadership was an act of generosity that inspired his team even more than his personal performance did. We hear a lot about the "greatest generation," which was defined by patriotism and great sacrifice. Phelps's sacrifice of his place in the final spotlight is perhaps indicative of another generation that is poised to carry on that kind of greatness, with the realization that giving people a gift is the way to change the outcome. At the end of the day, people become true leaders because they are willing to give of themselves. They make generosity their practice.

PEOPLE

Checklist for Leaders

Practice/Activity

❑ **Be the Leader**
Hire people *you* personally would follow.

❑ **Be the Director of Education**
Teach your people all the time and encourage others to do the same.

❑ **Be a Motivator . . . Through More Hard Work**
Work hard to get the best out of your people.

❑ **Have the Courage to Tell It Straight**
Reward great performers. Be direct and honest with underachievers.

❑ **Trust Your Gut Instincts**
Learn what your people value.

CHAPTER 2

PURPOSE

Before You Set Sail,
Know Your Direction

We succeed only as we identify in life, or in war, or in anything else,
a single overriding objective, and make all other considerations
bend to that one objective.—DWIGHT D. EISENHOWER

I'm back on my home turf of New York City and it feels good. This morning Jonathon and I are walking through Central Park watching moms push their strollers and street vendors set up their hot dog carts. I'm in the hiking shoes I bought for my North Carolina trek. They seem a bit out of place here, but more comfortable than loafers once they're broken in. I guess when it comes to treading lightly, it still is a possibility to teach an old foot some new tricks. (Hah!)

Usually at this time of the early morning, I'm heading downtown, checking voice mails, and preparing for the coming day's appointments and meetings. Taking the time to step out of my usual routine and habits while here in my home city is a real gift. I can't help but ask myself, do routines have meaningful purpose or are they simply habits picked up over time? Have you noticed that when you ask people how it's going at work, nine times out of ten they say, "Busy!" That has become our mantra for letting others know how successful we are. But consider why is it that when the most successful people in the world meet with you they seem to have all the time in the world? They never seem to look at their watch or look past you. People like that seem to work outside time.

It appears that what they experience are focused moments of purposeful engagement that flow one into the other. They have a unique ability to concentrate on the present task at hand, and it gives them, and you, energy.

Being back in the city after being in Jon's neck of the woods makes me feel the sheer mass energy of it, the chaotic dynamism that collides and bounces off everyone, like electrons bouncing off a nucleus. Everyone seems ready for action—prepared for something to happen. Going somewhere! But where are they going? From this park lens, looking at this early-bird scene of speed and bustle, it's as if everyone has a prescribed mission they were given this morning, and perish the thought that they might look up or even speak until after that mission is achieved. If all these people I'm watching whiz by me truly had a sense of purpose, I'd say, "Wow, with that kind of drive, they could power the world and cure cancer in one fell swoop." Yet plenty of people don't know where they're going—they don't know which stop is for them. This is the unfortunate direction for too many people: They go along for the ride, without having taken the time to chart a clear course. Jonathon loves to say that Nietzsche reminds us of this all the time: "Once you know the why you can figure out any how." The question is, Do you know the "why"?

Many times I've found it is a lot more important to know what the right questions are than the right answers. Jon talks about how in Zen, the question often already contains the answer. Jon's idea is that you do not pick your purpose as much as that your purpose picks you.

A great purpose is dynamic—it is a vision that can grow to

> ## *Jon:*
>
> *Figuring out the* why *constitutes a training of the will such that obstacles become temporary points of learning, not things that actually stop us from realizing our destiny. Nietzsche was insistent that we not settle for easy answers brought down from the mounts of tradition. He wanted us to struggle to find our own answers—to know them from within.*

meet the demands of the moment. Without creating a differentiating purpose, a leader is only a force of personality rather than an agent of change. Without a clear purpose that followers can buy into, the institution will eventually fail.

When I was recruited in August 1988 to the Robert A. Becker advertising agency, I didn't know that our Merck, Sandoz, and Pfizer business was about to walk out the door. But within ninety days those clients were gone and the agency was down to thirty people. The holding company's management said to me: "Look, just get us back into the black. Just present our board with a solid vision and a plan for execution and we'll buy into it." Fast forward to 2003 and we win the "Agency of the Year" award. We have 320 people and Becker has seven of the top ten pharmaceutical companies as clients representing more billion-dollar-plus products than any ad agency in history. When I reflect back on how we made that happen, it comes down to a distinctive purpose, plain and simple, and getting our key people to buy into it. That vision was to create a company that can drive client brands beyond expectation, and focus solely on building blockbuster products better than anyone else. If we could do that (I thought) they will come—both clients and great employees—and we did and they did. We didn't single-aim our effort on advertising or direct marketing; we focused on whatever strategy could drive the client's products to their highest outcome.

On the other side of this mission of building products to exceed the expectations of our advertising agency clients was the product itself and the company the product comes from. When Gerald (Jerry) Belle came to speak at the Fordham Leadership Forum, he expanded my thinking (and that of my students) on how global companies can coalesce and move in a unified direction through openness. It's quite a skill to merge products, product management, sales forces, and customer interests when they all are located in one geography. Just think what a major task that becomes when global entities merge through acquisition. There's even a subspecialty in consulting called "post-merger integration" that deals with this very phenomenon.

In class, Belle spoke convincingly that leadership at a global (and I'll add domestic) organization includes the ability to transcend political and cultural differences and bring people together under the same roof for a common cause. As former leader of Aventis (now Sanofi-Aventis) for North America, Belle headed a large company that is a well-respected tapestry of many cultures that have been successfully sewn together. That's no mean feat these days, when most mergers fail to strengthen organizations and often dilute their purpose. With his company the result of a merger between a French pharmaceutical company (Rhône-Poulenc Rorer) and a German one (Hoechst Marion Roussel), Belle told the Forum that despite differences in culture, political orientation, and other general matters, people pulled together—putting all their effort into inventing and selling pharmaceuticals that save people's lives everywhere. To a great extent, Belle credits good, consistent communication for the positive results.

Belle has worked all over the world and is an impressive communicator, not because he overpowers you, but because he stands back and listens. After all, the power of communication is more than words; it is openness. When it comes to talking, Belle is known for expressing his purpose through his skills in conversation, jesting, persuasion, even taking his purpose to the bully pulpit to convince his corporate and global cohorts to recognize the bigger picture and the mission to be fulfilled. He makes the art of communication an integral part of company culture, and that is how different notions, styles, and traditions get successfully blended into one purpose.

Just recently, Belle accepted the role of executive chairman for Merial Ltd., a large multibillion-dollar animal health business that is itself the result of a joint venture between Sanofi-Aventis and Merck & Co. There, he again finds himself stressing the positives of openness and communication as Merial employees strive to make their goal of bringing good health to animals a reality.

Why does one firm succeed and another fail? I think the difference comes down to communicating the company's vision on a continual basis and doing what you need to do to get your people to buy into it. A well-communicated vision answers the question behind the question. "Why do we come to work every day? What's our job? Is it just to make money?" Well, if it were just to make money, why would you care where you worked? For many others, including me, it is purpose that separates one company from another. People want to work in places where they can buy into the company's vision and leave their own personal legacy of success.

The story of Mary Kay Ashe, a woman in her late forties in the 1950s and the founder of Mary Kay Cosmetics, exemplifies the 360-degree possibilities in having a differentiated purpose. Ashe got ordinary, plain-looking women to consider using her products through one-to-one evangelical selling. As a result, these women

---

Jon:

In Zen terms, it is not so much about gaining your will as giving it up. What I mean is that you must let go of the grip of ego that is pushing you to a purpose—what you think you "should do"—and instead give over to the inward stillness beyond ego. Zen says strive to accept your "Big Mind" that leads you to a purpose well beyond what you once rationally imagined.

---

looked and felt better than they ever had in their lives, and here's the genius—she gave those women something to do with the energy of those feelings. Ashe created a housewife workforce that said, "I love these products. I'm going to sell these products. They've transformed me. And I'm going to personally get the word out and recruit other people like myself to sell these products." Ashe's secret was to recruit salespeople who were not hired mercenaries but rather true believers. Ashe created the evangelical sales force, a wholly new concept—she was a brilliant pioneer.

MAKE IT BIG

Make it something beyond the everyday . . . something that is a way of life, not merely a goal.

John Glenn is somebody who has always had a very clearly stated purpose for his life. Glenn set deliberate goals for himself as a Marine pilot, a test pilot, an astronaut, and a senator. As a Marine pilot in World War II, he flew fifty-nine combat missions; in Korea, he flew sixty-three. Glenn was awarded the Distinguished Flying Cross on six occasions and holds the Air Medal with eighteen Clusters for his service during WWII and Korea.

As a test pilot, Glenn set a transcontinental speed record in 1957 flying from Los Angeles to New York in three hours and twenty-three minutes. Glenn joined NASA in 1959 and became an astronaut. In 1962, aboard the *Friendship 7,* he was the first American to orbit the earth. In a four hour, fifty-five minute mission, Glenn orbited the earth three times at an average speed of 17,500 miles per hour. He went on to a distinguished career in the U.S. Senate starting in 1974 that lasted for twenty-four years. And it was on October 29, 1998, that Senator John Glenn, at age 77, returned to space on board the space shuttle *Discovery.*

This time Glenn went up for a nine-day mission where he orbited the earth 134 times at an altitude of 350 statute miles. The mission was a great success, and among other scientific breakthroughs accomplished aboard it, Glenn was able to participate in a study that has greatly served the forward progress of understanding how we age.

After doing so much, what could possibly be left to do for Senator Glenn? Glad you asked. Not long after John Glenn got back down on the ground, he founded the John Glenn Institute for Public Service and Public Policy, housed at the Ohio State University in Columbus. Glenn got involved with the institute for the same reason he did all of the other things over the course of his life—to live his purpose, to serve a country that he believed in and loved.

John Glenn's new purpose in life was to provide an environment where college students from around the country could come to study public policy and learn how to make informed, thoughtful decisions about how the government could best serve the public good. Nothing bothered him more when he was in the Senate than when public officials would lose sight of what was good for their constituencies. Glenn wanted to train future leaders from a nonpartisan perspective—he wants to teach young people that government can work, that thoughtful inquiry can take precedence over partisan opinion.

Eighty-three now and in fabulous shape, Glenn has not wavered in his commitment to his purpose. It has grown ever stronger as the need for nonpartisan, thoughtful consideration of public policy has increased. While growing up in the small town of Concord, Ohio, listening to his father's stories of World War I, the burning question for John Glenn was always the same. "How do I serve this great country that I love and whose values I believe are worth upholding?" That question required Glenn to make his life as a leader the answer.

MAKE IT INCLUSIVE

*Make sure every key customer and person in
the organization has a place at the table.*

Bill Shore, the executive director of Share Our Strength, had to bring a lot of people to his table when he declared almost twenty-five years ago that the purpose of his organization would be to end world hunger. People thought he was crazy. Ending world hunger is something a kid collecting pennies around the neighborhood says, not a savvy chief of staff for a prominent senator (Gary Hart) and later manager of Hart's presidential campaign. But Shore said it and has been living it for the last quarter century.

Shore reaches out to high-profile chefs around the world and convinces them that they could be big contributors to stopping hunger if they would do what they do best: prepare their signature dishes to be served, accompanied by great wine, at top-dollar fundraisers in beautiful locales. Share Our Strength organizes the gala events and then donates the proceeds to organizations that have proven track records of fighting hunger in the United States and abroad. The events have become so prestigious and well attended that some companies pay Share Our Strength as much as $2 million every year for the privilege of being co-sponsors.

Shore's innovative approach to ending world hunger opens a place at the table not just for those interested in the nonprofit sector, but also for those who want to do something socially positive and at the same time improve their own bottom line by gaining notice for their brand. Shore makes good use of for-profit corporations and their need to increase product visibility through positive image building. He does not exclude any organization that comes to the table to support the larger purpose of ending hunger. Share Our Strength helped build the image of the Evian brand of bottled water, and simultaneously brought in $2 million to the larger purpose of ending hunger.

How does Shore succeed in including so many different players in his purpose, and keeping them inspired and encouraged? How does he do it in a field where long hours, low pay, and not enough results have traditionally burned people out?

By cross-fertilizing private-sector business building with nonprofit missionary zeal, Shore has created a business whose purpose is inclusive and breathes new positives into both sectors. Nonprofit and for-profit businesses have a lot to learn from each other and a lot of ways they can help each other. Since Share Our Strength began, it has raised more than $150 million to end hunger. Has hunger disappeared? No. But the purpose has given birth to an entire movement that incorporates business purpose under the umbrella of social purpose and breeds the kind of inclusion that keeps organizations alive and growing.

STAY MISSION-CENTERED

Don't let the daily grind divert you from the matter at hand—stay close to the purpose of your organization.

Mayor Rudy Giuliani called Howard Safir New York's best police commissioner. Over the course of his career, Safir has led four of the largest government/municipal organizations in the world and transformed all of them. Safir is successful because he is an agent of change—a leader who lives his purpose daily for all to see. Having graduated 187 out of 188 in his high school senior class in the Bronx, Safir likes to tell the story about his guidance counselor telling him, "Howard, the world needs truck drivers." But he went to college anyway to play football. And after being away from home and substantially on his own, he decided his purpose was law enforcement. After college, he got an opportunity to work undercover for the U.S. Drug Enforcement Administration (DEA), where he stayed for seven years.

It is kind of funny now to think of this imposing, straight-arrow, rock-solid, former NYC police and fire commissioner as an undercover agent in the 1960s, sporting a long beard and ponytail and robed in a "toga," as he called it. He made more cases than anyone undercover in the DEA at the time. Like I said, Howard Safir lived his purpose daily and still does today.

Safir talks a lot about the necessity of staying mission-oriented despite the minutiae large government organizations present. When he was undercover, there was the typical "them and us" attitude between agents in the field and the "suits" at headquarters. Most agents thought the suits didn't know a thing about the street, and most suits thought the agents on the street didn't know a thing about strategy. But Howard Safir never gets bogged down in those kinds of debates. For him, it's the mission that matters—locking up criminals. As he puts it, "Good leaders are mission-oriented and see what the goal is. You can't get bogged down in bureaucracy or tradition. Leaders don't continue bad policies." So after seven years undercover, he shaved off his beard, cut off his ponytail, put on a suit, went down to headquarters, and applied for a job in the DEA as an internal strategist, a job where he managed agents on the street. Turned down at first, he persisted, knowing this job would be the best and fastest route to his purpose—which was assuming a leadership role.

Later, Safir wound up leading and transforming the United States Witness Protection Program, the United States Marshals Service, the New York City Fire Department, and the New York City Police Department. Every job built more credibility for the next one. When he was assigned to head up the Witness Protection Program (WPP), a branch of the U.S. Marshals Service, it was in a state of disaster. After Safir interviewed the most highly regarded of his new employees (this "orientation" interviewing is something a lot of great leaders do, and always one-on-one), he learned that no one working at WPP wanted to be there—that they in fact abhorred the people they were being paid to protect. Safir decided to help every disgruntled employee get reassigned, and he brought in fresh, unjaded personnel who would commit to the agency's purpose, one that the leader himself had some difficulty coming to terms with at first.

After all, Safir put criminals away for a living. Why would he now want to shelter them, give them money, and provide them the essentials of a new life? Because he saw the big picture, and that meant that bringing the worst lawbreakers to justice involved protecting and even coddling other criminals who helped make the case. He worked hard to get buy-in from WPP agents, to encourage that they view their role as part law enforcement officer, part social worker. Isn't a small child innocent, even a criminal's child? Safir told his people to make that child the thread that wove purpose into their job. His relentless focus on mission over minutia helped mold a department that felt purposeless into one that was steeped in a sense of purpose.

CREATE MEANING

It must make sense to everyone—work hard for their buy-in.

Once Safir saw concrete evidence that his people were committed, he fought for them to get raises. Eventually, the WPP became the highest-paid branch of the U.S. Marshals Service. Before Safir came on board, they had been the lowest paid. He also arranged for them to receive special training in order to be qualified to provide the security for the United Nations General Assembly special sessions held once a year. At one time the lowest on the totem pole, with their self-esteem in the gutter, the WPP agents were now the ones designated to protect 130 of the world's most important leaders.

Howard Safir teaches us the importance of making people stretch into a clearly defined purpose bigger than their initial view, and once they buy in, rewarding them in a way that creates a deeper sense of meaning in their lives.

One final Safir saga: In 1995, New York City had the highest cardiac arrest fatality rate in the United States. It took emergency medical services (EMS) eight and a half minutes to respond to a cardiac call. After eight minutes you're brain dead. FDNY Commissioner Safir had an idea. He knew 80 percent of a firefighter's time is spent sitting in the firehouse waiting for the bell to ring, and he also knew his average firefighter's response time was four minutes. Couldn't the firefighters administer cardiac aid and save more lives?

At Safir's urging, firefighters were trained as certified first responders skilled in using defibrillators. Cardiac arrest fatalities in the city dropped dramatically and Safir made sure that firefighter salaries went up. For their additional training and services, he did not just get them a raise, but $1,500 more than police officers—and in New York City, that's a big deal because it is about pride. Through his leadership and by making firefighters an integral part of reducing cardiac arrest deaths, Safir created meaning for the entire department. You have to know what means a lot to your people and when they commit wholeheartedly to a collective purpose, reward them personally.

Purpose is often personal. Fires are dangerous and their threat is immediate. "I've been putting out fires all morning" has become a common metaphor for crisis management. Jamie Huysman is a "firefighter," but not a typical one. Jonathon introduced me to Huysman's work as an unconventional example of purpose, and I found its message quite relevant. A licensed clinical social worker (LCSW) and doctor of psychology (PsyD), Huysman has been a therapist dealing with patients in emotional crisis for over twenty years. An expert in his field, Huysman was featured, at one time, on the *Geraldo* show.

From that experience Huysman saw new hope for troubled people: that television, properly used, could open people's minds to admitting problems and asking for and receiving help. But he quickly realized that this process also allowed people to be seduced into airing their traumas and dramas for a waiting TV audience and that it was producing more harm than good.

He observed that people who appeared on these shows were often there as a last resort. Instead of help, they received voyeuristic judgment from a national audience ready to be entertained and a "clinical triggering" of their challenging psychological issues to return home with. Just sending people who had appeared on the shows home without professional follow-up was creating a liability for guests, their families, and even the shows. For a therapist whose personal mission was to do away with the shame and stigma of mental health issues, the situation became untenable.

As a response, Huysman founded TV Aftercare, a national network of hospitals, outpatient programs, and therapists created to serve people who first aired their problems on television. In concert with more than ten different talk, court, and reality shows over a twelve-year period, the organization has, to date, helped more than 600 families receive more than $6 million in free therapeutic care.

One important television show that steadily used the services of TV Aftercare and remained committed to healing, not simply entertaining, was *The Leeza Show*. The host, Leeza Gibbons (of *Entertainment Tonight* fame), and Jamie Huysman formed a special relationship during the show's six-year run. Gibbons experienced a personal crisis in her own life when her mother was diagnosed with early-onset Alzheimer's at age 57. Besides the suffering her mother experienced directly, the disease took a tremendous toll on family members. Gibbons turned to Huysman for help.

Being a woman of action and wanting to use her "celebrity" to help others, Gibbons created the Leeza Gibbons Memory Foundation and serves as the organization's chairman. Jamie Huysman took up the helm of executive director and began establishing Leeza's Places all over the country. These are sites where people with

Alzheimer's and other memory disorders and their caregivers can go to receive support from others, create a scrapbook of memories of their loved ones, and produce a memory-rich documentary film. The guiding principle of these living room–like welcome zones is "education, empowerment, and energy."

Jamie Huysman is a leader who gets things done with incredible business and broadcast savvy, as well as the utmost compassion. His talent is his ability to make a connection to the heart, and such a skill can never be underestimated. His focus on helping people with their personal pain might well be one of the most crucial parts of a leader's job—providing others a way to work through what once paralyzed them. The Leeza Gibbons Memory Foundation stays intimate with its purpose precisely because its impetus was founded on a personal story with universal application. By sharing her own personal story, Gibbons helps other caregivers get in touch with what is most personally important to them. This unique organization demonstrates a great lesson—purpose is personal!

CHECK IT OFTEN

Is it still vital? If not, change it to make it so.

Management guru Peter Drucker tells leaders that if the purpose of their organization is no longer connecting with the people, then it is time to let go and change. Drucker calls this process "planned abandonment." It's the notion that in organizations, things are dynamic and need to interact with the real world in real time. If decisions don't have "cash value" on the street, it is time to abandon out-of-date policies, procedures, or requirements. To keep purpose vital, it's essential to check and recheck if your purpose is forwarding your organization. Where do you go for these checkups? To your customers, constituents, students, and, of course, to the people charged with carrying out your purpose on a daily basis.

As Bill Toppeta of MetLife says, "You have to love what you do, and if you don't, you have to have the courage to find a new purpose." Toppeta told me that he keeps a physical object, a canoe paddle, in his office as a talisman of the importance he places on people working toward the same purpose. It's a reminder that if all the people in the boat are not rowing in the same direction, the boat just goes in circles.

This is one of the things that keeps Bill Toppeta on the road so much—he says you can never underestimate the power of communication. He got his first insight into that when he was still a newbie at MetLife (he's been there over thirty years). One of the higher-ups came to him, put a hand on his shoulder, and said, "You're doing a great job; we're all happy about it. Keep up the good work." Toppeta says as a young staffer, that comment was worth more than money to him and it made him work doubly hard. This early interaction taught Toppeta the importance of personal feedback with the people who work for you.

Personal communication keeps a purpose vital in two directions. First, from the leader to the direct report, it allows the direct report to learn how what she is personally doing is connected to the overall purpose of the larger organization. And from the direct report back to the leader, it allows the leader to hear if the individual charged with executing the organization's goals still relates to the purpose. It also allows the leader to learn from the people on the front line whether the purpose developed at headquarters has relevance. If not, then "planned abandonment" is in order and a new purpose needs to evolve.

The likes of Bill Toppeta, Bill Shore, Mary Kay Ashe, John Glenn, and Howard Safir remind us that purpose is not something set in stone to hang framed on a wall. Purpose has to be alive with vitality and should move people into their best future as it sustains them in a challenging and creative present. If it is not doing that, then it's time to scrap it and find a new purpose.

Life is change, and letting go of our "sacred cow" is sometimes the most energizing thing we can do in an organization. The minute we begin loving our missions blindly and can no longer objectively see the real world in which that mission must be carried out—and the real people who must carry it out—we are not leaders anymore. We have become status quo managers. Vital leaders pay attention to the pulse of the purpose and respond quickly to revive it when it's in cardiac arrest.

Jonathon's Perspective

In the world to come, I shall not be asked, "Why were you not Moses?"
I shall be asked, "Why were you not Zusya?
—Rabbi Zusya

I have many Post-it notes with quotes on them that live on my desk. This one from Rabbi Zusya is an old favorite. Something I discovered more recently that has meant a lot to me is an affirmation from Howard Thurman. Thurman was an activist for civil rights before there was an official movement. He met Gandhi in 1936 and was forever changed. His grandmother, an ex-slave, raised him and he went on to get his PhD in religious studies and serve as president of Howard University. He later became the founder of the first fully integrated church in the United States. "Don't worry about what the world needs," said Thurman, "ask what makes you come alive and do that. Because what the world needs are people who have come alive." To me, this is the sentiment my father is expressing in this chapter. It is the process by which leaders come to purpose, not necessarily the content of their purpose, that is of the essence in the study of leadership. I couldn't agree more.

I don't think it is possible to have a purpose imposed on you from the outside and make it your own. For a purpose to be authentic, it has to rise up from inside you. Finding a purpose that is considered objectively "good" is irrelevant if that purpose has nothing to do with your talents and passion.

This is why I have always liked Rabbi Zusya's imagining of what God will ask him when he enters heaven—not why wasn't he more like Moses, but why he wasn't more Zusya-like. We are each different and have a unique place and purpose in the world. Often the head points to what society calls objectively "good." But when we follow this ideal alone, we may be thought of as "good" by our peers and parents, getting accolades for our choices, while we suffer internally. What matters is that the person doing the work feels a sense of purpose, not drudgery and obligation.

John Glenn made his choice and it is awesome and intimidating. But remember he didn't do it solely because of duty. He wanted to fly higher and faster than anyone else. And the same for Howard Safir, whose story also seems like an impossible thing to live up to. Don't live up to it. Don't ask yourself why you're not more like John Glenn or Howard Safir. Ask why you're not more like yourself.

There is a Zen story that Zen teacher Cheri Huber tells about a woman who goes to a monastery to attend her first retreat. She is feeling very holy about this experience, like it is really something special. She sees the Zendo (a place for meditation) and sees how beautiful and silent it is, and she feels privileged to be there. Upon entering the Zendo the first morning, she notices a bucket filled with a soiled mop and dirty water just outside the door. She walks passed it, but observes she is feeling angry that it is there. Because it is a silent retreat, no one talks to her, but she finds the voices inside her head going wild wanting that bucket gone. Every day for five days she focuses on the bucket being there, and it ruins all of her meditations as she becomes more and more internally furious with the monks for ruining her peace with this horrible sight of the mop and bucket. "Somebody should move that bucket and clean it!" she hears herself thinking. Finally, on the sixth morning, the voice inside her head says: "Wait a minute, you're somebody." And after internalizing that insight, she picked up the bucket, cleaned it out, and put it away.

We are all somebody. And we can all move to lead anytime we choose. Safir graduated 187 out of 188 students in his high school class. It would have been real easy for him to take his guidance counselor's advice and become a truck driver, because the counselor was right—the world does need truck drivers. And some people find their purpose in that profession and make it possible for all the rest of us to have the goods we take for granted every day. But the counselor was wrong about one crucial detail—the world did not need Howard Safir to be a truck driver. The world needed him as a leader in law enforcement. But that truth came later. At the time, all Safir knew was that he had a desire to become something else. He listened to his gut and had the courage to follow. This is all we can do.

After we have made the choice to follow our gut and become leaders as a result, how do we then make room for those working for us to do the same? This is a critical question. There are plenty of people out there who get wrapped up in their own cause to the exclusion of others. To this point, I think my father's story of Bill Shore at Share Our Strength is a good model. Shore didn't want the people who come to work for him simply to mimic his purpose; he wanted them to delve into their own. Shore is a thinker/doer, and he wants his people to be thinkers/doers, too. Shore knows that personal internal commitment is the only thing that really sustains people over the long term and that anything else is only a temporary show.

In his *Letters to a Young Poet,* Rainer Maria Rilke advises the young man writing him to "live your questions now, and perhaps even without knowing it, you will live along some distant day into your answers." Great leaders like John Glenn and the rest mentioned by my father want the same thing for their followers that Rilke wanted for the young poet he was trying to help along into adulthood. They want the people working for them to heed the purpose inside them through the struggle of figuring it out for themselves. True leaders are smart enough to know that anything else won't do.

Mack Pearsall, chairman of the North Carolina Institute of Political Leadership, told me that knowledge is the serial elimination of illusion. I would say this is true for self-knowledge as well. Growing up entails letting go of the illusion of what you think you are and instead focusing your energies on being exactly who you are. When you settle into who it is you actually are, rather than what you think you should be, unique things occur.

Nancy Lublin is the founder of Dress for Success, a national organization that provides job interview and business attire for women who could not otherwise afford it. She is a great example of a young person who lived her question fully—right into her answer. Lublin was a twenty-four-year-old law student in New York City ten years ago and hated it. She was in law school for the same reason that lots of us do things—inertia. She opened her mailbox one day to find a $5,000 check from her great grandfather's estate. It surprised her because he had died a while back and she didn't expect anything. But when she saw the check, a flood of memories about her great grandfather returned. He had been an immigrant to the United States, lived to provide for his family, and worked hard to send his children to college. Lublin recollected her great grandfather was a man who worked hard for every penny and wanted his money to be used to give his family a better life.

By the time Lublin rode up the elevator the six floors to her Manhattan apartment, the "Dress for Success" idea was there in her mind—her purpose had found her. A new car or more clothes or furniture for her apartment would not make her life at law school any better; a life-lifting purpose was the thing that would change her life.

With her family not totally in favor of the idea, Lublin went to see one of her professors, who advised her to seek out some nuns she knew of in the Spanish Harlem section of New York City. Lublin found the nuns and told them of her desire to start a program where well-off businesswomen who discard clothes every season would have a place where they could donate those almost-new clothes to homeless and low-income women. For these women, the barrier to landing a job and getting back on their feet was that they did not have the appropriate work attire. The nuns were enthusiastic.

She shared with the nuns the story about her great grandfather, and about how she had allocated her whole $5,000 inheritance to get the concept off the ground. She asked the nuns for help in connecting her with the women who could benefit. Convinced of how committed and dedicated Lublin was, they helped her to begin. As they say, the rest is history.

Nancy Lublin opened clothing intake centers throughout the city and later the entire country. Dress for Success has become a favorite charity and philanthropic resource for working women who want to give back to their community and offer other women a leg up. As you probably guessed, Lublin withdrew from law school (though she eventually got her degree) and ran Dress for Success full-time.

Today, Lublin is CEO of an organization called Do Something.

Its mission is helping high school students to do charitable and community-oriented "good deeds." Lublin found that making the leap to live your life with purpose and passion is easier than thinking about it day after day. She no longer found herself struggling with the question of what to do; she just started doing.

My dad wrote about the bustle we saw in New York City as we roamed around waxing on about purpose. In the fall of last year, I had a very different walking experience. I went on a Zen walking meditation retreat on the Appalachian Trail led by Zen teacher Shohaku Okamura. The walk was supposed to be silent, but he did give one instruction before our group of twelve started out. Okamura said simply, "Slow walkers in front." I didn't realize why until later. Okamura wanted us to notice the forest and to notice ourselves in the forest. Okamura walked at the back of the group—a very different image from the traditional notion of "follow the leader." His leadership message was elegantly clear: "Don't follow me; instead learn to trust the process of following your own lead and purpose will emerge."

Christopher Reeve died as we were writing this chapter. To my mind, his life had a purpose before he fell off that horse, and it had a purpose when he figuratively got back on. The man single-handedly changed the way we think about spinal cord injury. He did it by lifting a finger. He did it by never giving up. Reeve did it by continuing to work, act, direct, and write. Reeve fervently believed that he would walk again. A month before he died, he appeared on *The Oprah Winfrey Show* and she asked him point blank: "What happens if you can never walk again?" Oprah asked the question haltingly, as if the thought itself would crush him. But this was Superman, and he answered, "Then I won't walk again." No big drama, no reason to stop fighting; it just means he won't walk. The possibility of failure does not mean you give up on your purpose, it just means you have looked at failure and have moved on.

PURPOSE

Checklist for Leaders

Practice/Activity

❑ **Make It Big**

Make it something beyond the everyday . . . something that is a way of life, not merely a goal.

❑ **Make It Inclusive**

Make sure every key customer and person in the organization has a place at the table.

❑ **Stay Mission-Centered**

Don't let the daily grind divert you from the matter at hand—stay close to the purpose of your organization.

❑ **Create Meaning**

It must make sense to everyone—work hard for their buy-in.

❑ **Check It Often**

Is it still vital? If not, change it to make it so.

CHAPTER 3

PASSION

A Fire That Warms

If passion drives you, let reason hold the reins.—BENJAMIN FRANKLIN

When Jon and I started talking about passion, my alma mater Ohio State University came to mind. It was where my early passion took fire—a school I loved because it taught this kid from Brooklyn so much about transformation. I relished the sports mania OSU stood for and the academic challenges it threw at me and the lifetime friends I made there. I had never thought of inviting Jon to come back with me to Ohio State. I always just thought it was just "my thing" and that he wouldn't find much use for it. Jon doesn't follow college football and rarely watches sports on TV, but he enjoys a good drama. And when he did finally join me at an OSU alumni weekend during the course of writing this book, that's exactly what he found the Ohio State football experience to be—high drama and full of passion.

The highlight before the game is when the "best damn band in the land" marches onto the field. In unison, the band performs "Script Ohio," where band members carrying their instruments do a syncopated march to form the word *Ohio* written as if in penmanship script. It is as though all individuals disappear and one word takes their place set to music. The pinnacle comes with the dotting of the "i" in Ohio. It is an honor normally given to the senior class tuba player. And yes, even Jon got swept away in it. And he didn't even go to school there, doesn't follow the team's win-loss record, and would rather listen to Dizzy Gillespie than John Philip Sousa any day . . . but it didn't matter.

The band's work ethic and flawless execution, its demonstration of a perfectly coordinated effort for a unified purpose, its pride and unflagging spirit—the passion got to him. We have to ask ourselves what we can learn from that kind of performance. Jon and I asked each other that question all weekend as we walked the campus and all over the city of Columbus discussing leaders who practice "passion" and inspire others to do and be more than they ever thought they could.

A working definition of *passion* is the practice of embracing your job and your organization with great vitality and commitment, creating a spark that ignites the spirit of your followers, and maintaining the will "to do it" better than it's ever been done before.

LOVE THE WORK

Is your focus on the work or the reward? If you can't answer "work," reevaluate what you do and where you are, and move on if necessary.

Bill Toppeta of MetLife told the Fordham Leadership Forum that you must love the job you're doing or find another. When he first

> ### *Jon:*
>
> *We entered the great cathedral (Ohio Stadium) known by its congregation as "the shoe." The famed "Script Ohio" was under way. As I watched the drum major, it occurred to me that this was like the queen bee leading a hive to enact its ordered dance of spring.*
>
> *At the game's end, the players huddled in the center of the field, removed their helmets, and made their way to the bandstand. There they sang the words to Ohio State's alma mater. I heard my dad's voice behind me.*
>
> *As we walked down a few flights, we mingled with 105,000 people going to their cars or out to the local bars. The band was on the field and still playing. The stadium was nearly empty, but the band played on—not for the sake of the audience but held there by the sheer passion of its performance.*

said that, and then later, when the class rated him so highly for passion, I thought it was interesting because Toppeta doesn't work in what you'd call a glamour industry. One doesn't ordinarily think of insurance as passionate work. But it's harder to make the argument stick when Toppeta talks about what provides the sustaining fuel for his passion: providing financial freedom to his clients.

Money by itself isn't enough of a motivator. Financial freedom implies a relief from stress, which is a worthy goal. I know this is a crucial point for Jon's generation and the millennials coming up behind him. There has to be meaning—a real purpose—because money just isn't enough. This stands in clear contrast to Wall Street of the 1980s and early 1990s, which was inhabited by lots of people with unbridled egomaniacal passion, not for their work, but for the money they could make. Wall Street back then and the Enron types who followed had passion, but not to lead; their passion was the mighty dollar—period.

In sharp contrast to this bent on money for money's sake is the leadership of the energetic Father Joseph M. McShane, president of Fordham University. We often think of passion as drive, as wanting to constantly do and be more. But McShane's passion is important for us to understand because he is a man who truly loves his work, without financial reward. McShane doesn't make any money. He draws no salary, no bonus. Every cent of his compensation goes to the church, which modestly supports him. McShane's aim is to do God's will, so wherever he is placed, he sees it as God's will and he gives his all to his assignment without question. The sentiments that he embraces regarding his work come from the gospels in Luke 12:48: "To those who much is given, much is expected." He also adheres to the creed of the Jesuits, his religious order, first spoken by Saint Ignatius: "the greatest good, for the greatest number, for the greatest glory of God." It's not something we typically think of in business when trying to make our revenue numbers for the year.

Fordham was the preeminent academic Catholic institution from the 1950s through the early 1980s. As president, McShane's passion is to reclaim Fordham's position and preeminence. McShane's dad knew it as that, so did his brothers, and so did he in his mythic memory of visiting the university's halls as a boy with his dad, who spent time telling him of the power of education. McShane's passion for this goal is like "the zeal of a convert." There are twenty-eight Jesuit colleges in the nation, and schools like Georgetown, Boston College, and Notre Dame all currently rank above Fordham, but that wasn't always the case. For Father McShane, Fordham will regain its place in the rankings or he will know the reason why.

McShane jokes that although he doesn't make a penny, he "loves money." He loves it because of what it can do for the future of Fordham and for the 70 percent of students who receive financial aid directly from the university. He wants Fordham always to remain a school that people in the lower tier of the economy (like his family was) can attend.

At the Forum one night, the class kept asking him questions about his beliefs on leadership. In his final comment, Father McShane summed it up this way: "Real simply, to be a leader means you can never demean anyone. You have to find that thing in them which is great, and bring it out." And then smiling broadly, he left. One of my students asked, "Does he mean that if we want to lead, we have to find what it is inside us that we love and go do it?" I nodded. Then I asked, "And why do you think he mentioned the importance of not demeaning anyone if you want to lead?" A small voice from the back of the room perked up—one I had hardly heard from all semester—and said softly, "Because you never quite know the passion that's inside another person until they one day let you in on the secret." And the class had its answer. *Love the work and be vigilant not to underestimate or put down another's ideas.* It's your job to cultivate and fan passion. To blow coldly on it is not the leader's job.

In today's workplace, people are finding novel ways to hook up with work that inspires their passion. Community internships, where executives are excused from work for four weeks to do community service, have become part of the menu of perquisites that large companies use to build employee loyalty. United Parcel Service (UPS) is a big proponent of community service, and both employees who participate and the company itself have benefited. The extracurricular service is noted by upper management and UPS gets high marks in the community for the good works of its volunteer interns.

Volunteerism is 65 million people strong in the United States, and it's not a new phenomenon. In a February 27, 2005, *New York Times* piece by Eilene Zimmerman on what has been called the "give-back, get-back trend" ("Doing Well in Your Career by Doing Good Outside It"), LaVerne Campbell, director of Volunteers of America, said people increasingly volunteer with specific projects in mind. About 90,000 of the organization's volunteers are college students, people looking for a career change and women reentering the workforce. "They volunteer where they have a passion and it leads them to a new job," said Campbell.

Many young people I come in contact with ask about tying their career objectives to a passion and I encourage them to do just that. There is a nationwide movement toward passionate volunteerism as evidenced by Monster.com, the leading job search site, joining with Idealist.org, which matches people with nonprofits, and BoardnetUSA.org, which connects nonprofit boards with potential board members. So, there are legitimate new ways for you to brand yourself as a caring, passionate, trustworthy employee.

BE INNOVATIVE

Allow your passion to ask "unreasonable"
things of yourself and your people.

We tend to think of passion as unbridled, something beyond the rational, and MetLife's Toppeta makes a very cogent case for being demanding. He told the Forum class to "be unreasonable. When they tell you it will take a week to do [a task], ask why it can't be done in a day. When they tell you it will cost a million dollars, ask why you can't do it for half a million. Be unreasonable!" Toppeta makes the case that if we are reasonable all the time, how would we ever innovate? Wouldn't we simply accept the status quo of the day? Without the passion of a Thomas Edison or a Martin Luther King, would new inventions and new ways of thinking ever come into existence? For Toppeta and many leaders, it's passion that drives progress.

Passion that leads to innovation happens in the world of scientific discovery every day. We heard this from the very passionate Dr. Nicolas Bazan, founder and director of the Louisiana State University Neuroscience Center of Excellence in New Orleans. Bazan partners with some of the greatest research minds in the world to create innovations in brain research. Over his last twenty years at the LSU Medical School, he has brought in more grants than anyone in the school's history and facilitated the establishment of fourteen research teams to execute work on multiple aspects of brain research. Bazan inspires his people and their support staff by his insistence on passionate execution. One unique aspect of Bazan's work is that although he is a research physician trained to gather and analyze data, he searches constantly for new and better ways to discover cellular mechanisms that are relevant to diseases and to test experimental drugs that he and his lab have invented. It is not theory that captures his imagination; he is not satisfied until it can be proved that the formulation he has in his hands is a possible answer to help suffering and afflicted patients in need of new medications.

Bazan's personal area of brain research includes Alzheimer's, epilepsy, stroke, age-related macular degeneration, traumatic head injury, and pain management. What frustrates him most is that today there are only treatments but no cures for the major brain diseases he is working on. This frustration burns in him to do things better every day and to make the breakthroughs that will lead to cures. He and his team have already come up with an experimental new drug that, if injected within the first two hours of a stroke, can slow down the process. He has been advocating for some time that ambulances carry this compound on board because of the elapsing time window. He and his team have also discovered a key internal natural mechanism in the brain that can protect neurons and help them to heal themselves—if this approach pans out in clinical trials, a new method for treating Alzheimer's is the hoped-for result.

Bazan's hunger for discovery is a lesson for leaders. He doesn't give up and makes it his practice to go beyond reasonable assumptions to get to the breakthrough compounds that halt the spread of disease.

MERGE THE PERSONAL WITH THE GLOBAL

Everyone in your company has personal passions. Find a place in your company mission to acknowledge them.

How does a leader allow for his people's personal passions? Are large corporations with massive bureaucracies and thousands of employees capable of acknowledging the personal? They don't have a choice. Talented people are leaving organizations in large numbers because the corporate structure is not accommodating or integrating or recognizing personal passion. The good news is that the great companies are starting to do something about it. And this denotes a big change in business ideology. My students got the message firsthand when Bill Toppeta told the Forum that "what you need to know as the leader is what motivates your people, not what motivates you."

To bring this philosophy into the corporate structure, Toppeta uses a very revealing yet simple exercise. He hands out a questionnaire to managers and their direct reports. The manager ranks the items on the page in the order of what she believes most and least stirs her direct reports' passions. At the same time, the direct report also ranks the items on the list. The lists are compared and then dialogue ensues. Toppeta tells us that, for the most part, managers do horribly on this exercise. They think they know what their people are passionate about, but they don't. But as these dialogues take place and the central issues are made clear, amazing things happen—people get to know each other as people, not simply as functions that help the department make its numbers every quarter. The result? The people working for Toppeta have a voice in where they can best make their personal contribution to the company. The outcome of marrying personal passions to company goals breeds deeper job satisfaction for employees and more profits for the company.

Bill Gray, president of Ogilvy & Mather New York, seconds Toppeta's point of view. At his top-ten advertising agency in Manhattan, Gray runs one of our industry's most successful creative enterprises, composed of 1,600 people. These creative and strategic folks are not an easy group to inspire. As New York City advertising people tend to be, they're a smart, stubborn, and take-no-prisoners kind of workforce. Gray's job is to get the best out of these high-fliers every day, and he does so by infusing the language of passion in all his dealings. He loves the quote attributed to the Emperor Napoleon that "leaders are dealers in hope." That's how he sees his role.

Gray also told the Fordham Leadership Forum class that for years he golfed with General Electric's legendary CEO, Jack Welch. That experience taught him heaps about passion, and that great leaders such as Welch give it a lot of consideration. Welch gave him this piece of advice: Be passionate all the time and know everyone's name, from bottom to top, and show you do, especially to the people who least expect you to know their name. Welch's point, Gray told us, was that a leader can use the language of passion to create the soul of a small company in the body of a giant. And that is a unique advantage in business.

Gray also evoked another lesson from Jack Welch, which is that there are three Es he leads by: energy, energize, and edge. That's a good definition of a passionate leader from one of America's most passionate of leaders.

Building on his comments about Welch, Gray said that he personally views leadership like a person on the field of battle, actively engaged in the war. He stayed with this description, telling the class that a leader needs to know his troops, treat them as colleagues, get out in the field, be next to them, and seek to understand how the people on the front lines deal with the challenges they're confronted with. Match your passion to theirs and let them see what you're all about. A leader's biggest mistake? Forgetting the troops on the ground. And not trusting that they are giving their heart and soul to the fight. Even if a course correction is indicated, there can be an enormous unforeseen negative effect on the results you produce if you make the correction without first assessing the work in progress. That's a passion evaporater. Creativity, Gray believes, is very important to the goals of leadership. Leaders need to face problems with creativity. And solve them with creativity, too. It's an essential ingredient in the recipe to build lasting passion. For Bill Gray, leadership must instill passion or you're not truly leading.

EXERCISE PERIPHERAL VISION

Focus does not mean single-mindedness.

What is true for me and, I have come to find out, for a lot of leaders is that we once thought leadership was about inspiring others to be passionate about the things that we were passionate about. I realize now that it's only a small portion of the passion thing. The larger wedge of the pie is about helping people to discover their own passions, and to then find a place for them where they can best express those passions within the context of the overall company mission. Listening to the leaders at the Forum, I have learned that great leaders need to be passionate about their work, but not so single-mindedly passionate that they can't see and make room for the differing passions of others.

Greg Young, the fortysomething CEO of CorePharma, spoke to the Forum about Mahatma Gandhi as an example of a great leader. Gandhi is not someone you think of in a business context, but then Young has a unique take on things like this. His point was that Gandhi struggled diligently not to get overly caught up in the passion of his mission. He did not want to show off his passion or be guilty of developing a sense of phony self-importance. Young admired Gandhi's self-restraint and realization that arrogance is the antithesis of leadership.

Gandhi had an overriding mission that he was fiercely passionate about. And at the same time, no one can deny that he had the flexibility and openness to make room for the passions of others to come into his vision. The subtitle of Gandhi's autobiography is, "The story of my experiments with truth." Although he was a worldwide spiritual leader followed by millions in his lifetime, Gandhi never proclaimed to have "the truth." He only claimed that he was passionately experimenting. In doing so, he created lots of room for others to get involved, to experiment with their own truths, and to join in a struggle that was bigger than any one individual.

From experiments come innovations. If you are constantly experimenting, you are constantly trying and discovering new things to be passionate about. I know that for me, if I don't learn something new every day, I get a little depressed. (I tell that truth to my people often.) The world is too wide-ranging not to be willing take some chances—daring ones if you have the courage. And to lead, you have to have the courage.

BE RESULTS-ORIENTED

Focus on the outcome, not what you are going through.

When I think of courage, someone who comes to mind immediately is the senior vice president and treasurer of PepsiCo, Lionel Nowell. Nowell is from Columbus and an Ohio State graduate. Some would attribute this early OSU influence as a builder of his success . . . I have my own corroborating theories on this subject.

Nowell's passion for excellence speaks for itself. He is in the top tier of a $27 billion public company, serves on some of the top industrial and academic boards in the world, and is one of the most respected financial strategists in business today. But besides the specifics of Nowell's daily work, he has made it a special mission to communicate the leadership principles he's embraced over the years to young people across the country.

Nowell's first principle of passionate leadership is to "maintain ownership of who and what you are." He believes that a leader never places his future in somebody else's hands—a leader maps his own future and follows it through. To paraphrase the Roman philosopher Seneca, "If you don't know where you are going, then any road will take you there." Nowell told the class that to be a successful leader, you have to go after your goals with a passion, because "the only person who can keep you from getting what you want out of life is *you*." He stresses two other key points about passionate leadership that he feels are essential. The first one is: Do not be afraid of change and risk, but embrace it. The second: Do

J o n :

I spent a month on the Lakota Sioux Rosebud Reservation in South Dakota when I was twenty as part of a program called "Nonviolent Alternatives." It was cosponsored by the Lisle Fellowship and the Gandhi Peace Foundation (GPF). European Americans, Native Americans, and Indians from India lived together in tepees, cooked together, did physical labor on the reservation, and learned up close about the Native American approach to life. Any decision the Lakota Sioux made for their community and land had to take not just the human community into account but also all "theospia," or all relations— which meant the trees, rocks, wolves, deer, hawks, etc. It was an incredibly holistic teaching about nonviolence. The authentic leadership I encountered from the Lisle Fellowship leader, Chris Klug, and the GPF leader, Ramesh, was one of deep respect. What struck me most as they tried to model a Gandhian approach to understanding a new culture was their ability to include the rest of us and to make a point to teach us that what they were doing was "nothing special." It was just what human beings do when they value others.

not discriminate when it comes to people; learn to be open to anyone who can help you. One of his key messages is to challenge young people not to limit themselves.

When he was a youngster, Nowell used to go with his father at night to help him on his second job, cleaning offices in the central business district of Columbus, Ohio. When his father wasn't looking, he would go inside the huge wood-paneled executive conference rooms: "I used to twirl around in those big leather overstuffed chairs dreaming about what the people who sat in those big chairs did, what kinds of decisions they made, and wondering who those decisions affected—I wanted to be one of those people." And now he is.

But how does an African-American kid from the poor side of Columbus who was the first in his family to go to college rise to the very pinnacle of corporate life? It's the question on the mind of lots of young people who want to do the same thing. When you meet Lionel Nowell, his very presence answers that question. His passion about being successful immediately says to you, "I can overcome anything and so can you."

Nowell believes you need to be passionate about your goals and establish a written action plan for what you want out of life, professionally and personally. His advice to young leaders about getting through tough obstacles: "Focus on what you're going to, and not on what you're going through." Being passionate about what you are trying to achieve is the difference between someone who becomes a successful leader and somebody who does not.

Another leader whose corporate and military record is a testament to Lionel Nowell's mantra of focusing on the goal in front of you rather than the obstacle of the moment is Randy Thurman, former USAF top gun pilot and instructor and today, CEO of VIA-SYS Healthcare. Thurman participated in a University of Pennsylvania leadership study that found the number-one factor in determining a leader is how a person deals with adversity. Does adversity break her, or does she use it as an opportunity to become more resourceful and determined?

If times are hard and you hear yourself saying, "I just don't have the passion right now to focus on what I'm going to, because what I'm going through is too difficult," Randy Thurman and Lionel Nowell would ask you to think again.

Nowell firmly believes that "life is not a lake, but a stream,"

Jon:

Our editor gave us a book while we wrote The 100-Mile Walk. *It was coauthored by an expert on executive leadership and an attorney and advocate for equal opportunity. I like what it says about giving up on having total control.*

"You cannot control what other people do or think, and you cannot control all events that touch you, but you can choose to control your emotional and intellectual responses."
From Cracking the Corporate Code, *by Price M. Cobbs and Judith L. Turnock*

meaning there is no place to stop and simply rest—the passion drives on. This is why his first point—do not be afraid of change and risk, embrace it and be passionate about your goals—is so crucial.

Passion is not a one-time event, but a lifelong practice. When you're young, without much to lose and everything to gain, taking risks feels easier. As we gain success, most of us want to hold on. An attitude like this, though understandable, is the antithesis of leading. Great leaders change before they are forced to—they are ever at the ready to step out of their personal and professional comfort zones to achieve the next goal. Passionate leaders do not seek to attain status quo in the job; rather, they embrace the idea that they will change many times throughout their careers. A wise leader—no matter what her age—knows the longer she waits to make a change, the more painful it will be for her, the people following, and the organization.

As we've seen, leaders are people of passionate action. And taking action means making decisions—constantly. These decisions will often be hard ones and mistakes will be made. If as a leader you are not making mistakes, it is a sign that you are not pushing or stretching yourself enough, not taking enough calculated risks to better achieve your own and your company's goals. I think the difference between a long-term successful leader and a one-time successful manager is that, although both are passionate and don't dodge risk, the leader also displays passion about learning from her mistakes and uses setbacks to put together a smarter plan for the next challenge. The leader knows that you have to be able to make better and better choices as you progress along the way.

Of course, the risk a leader takes does not mean jumping out of a plane without a parachute. A leader's risk is calculated and leveraged against careful planning and a thorough understanding of the marketplace, the organization, and the financials. Knowing you will never have 100 percent of all the information you'd like, passion means that you make the decision anyway based on your gut intuition. Decisions to move forward are made not only because the data lines up the right way, but because behind every great decision is a leader who had the passion and the boldness to try something she believed would move the organization forward. Passion is what tips the scales for leadership. There are plenty of talented technicians, statisticians, and market research people, but the leader is the one who ultimately pulls the trigger and is held accountable. It takes a bellyful of passion to do that.

At the end of his leadership talk, Lionel Nowell read the Fordham MBAs a poem by James Patrick Kinney called "The Cold Within." The poem is about a group of five people sitting around a dying fire in the bitter cold; one is black, one poor, one rich, one of the church, and one bent on doing something for someone else only if it was first done for him.

The poem recounts how each person was holding tight to a single stick of wood rather than trying to keep the fire stoked. The rich person won't give up her stick of wood for the sake of the poor person. The poor person won't give up his wood because it might help the rich person. The black not for the white. The white not for the black. The person of the church not for the person outside the church, and the person who only gives if he is given to first refuses to give for the sake of others. The result: All the people around the fire freeze to death.

For Nowell, a leader must be the first one to throw his stick of wood onto the fire so that others can see how passion can ignite and take hold. A leader has to trust to be trusted. As this poem so aptly demonstrates, when divisiveness wins out, the passion of an organization flickers and dies. Great leaders build a fire where everybody can come and be warmed—and they must always be the first to throw in their kindling.

Jonathon's Perspective

> When genuine passion moves you, say what
> you've got to say, and say it hot.
> —D. H. LAWRENCE

I pointed the car west, then north, and Tennessee gave way to Kentucky. My father had been surprised when I told him I was driving rather than flying to Columbus to meet him for the football game; but when I looked at the map and saw that my trip would take me through Kentucky, I knew I had to stay on the ground. I had spent many summers traveling America and working along the way. Somehow, I had missed Kentucky. When I hit the state line, I thought of whiskey and bluegrass. I stopped to eat catfish and fried okra. The accents of the waitresses were thick and hard—their words clicked into each other like gears that turned my wheel in the exact direction it needed to go.

Once I got to Columbus, Dad told me that we were going to the time capsule ceremony at Ohio State's John Glenn Institute for Public Service and Public Policy, where we could put objects in the capsule that would be dug up 100 years from now. As Senator Glenn was speaking, I thought of the full lunar eclipse that was coming and of *Voyager One,* 8.4 billion miles from the sun, poised to leave our solar system. When John Glenn speaks, your mind turns to new worlds.

It took me thirty-five years to get to Columbus. Perhaps I wasn't ready until then to see my father's beginnings. But now that I have, I see that it is here, in this town named for the man who discovered America, that my father discovered himself. For a son to get a glimpse of the place in which his father discovered himself is a strange thing because in some way that you can't quite explain, that place has gotten into you long before you set foot in it. It made sense that it would be in this city and on this campus that we would discuss what Dad considers to be the fuel of leadership—passion.

I find myself incredibly inspired by the stories in this chapter. Passion, or love for what you do, is a leader's lifeblood. A big part of what's being said here is that if you don't feel overwhelming passion for it, you shouldn't stay where you are. Love it or find something else you do love. In this vein, my father built a company. Lionel Nowell rebuilt one. Bill Gray inspires major creative players in the advertising field. Father McShane aims to return a university that he loves to a place of preeminence in the world. Nicolas Bazan built a world-renowned neuroscience center and works daily to cure the brain's most daunting diseases.

The *Dhammapada,* the oldest known recorded sayings of the Buddha, puts it this way: "Your work is to discover your work, and then with all your heart, to give yourself to it." We have to be on the lookout, seeking where and when our opportunity will come to lead in that work that we feel has chosen us. Like Father McShane told the Fordham MBAs, everyone has a burning passion, and what they need most of all is a place to put it to use.

Think of Lionel Nowell going from helping his father clean boardrooms to being the one who sits on the boards. Think of all these leaders whose passion grew far beyond their own individual sense of triumph. Though many in their positions would have stopped there, these leaders were able to actualize their passion through developing others, not just themselves.

PASSION

Checklist for Leaders

Practice/Activity

❑ **Love the Work**

Is your focus on the work or the reward? If you can't answer "work," reevaluate what you do and where you are, and move on if necessary.

❑ **Be Innovative**

Allow your passion to ask "unreasonable" things of yourself and your people.

❑ **Merge the Personal with the Global**

Everyone in your company has personal passions. Find a place in your company mission to acknowledge them.

❑ **Exercise Peripheral Vision**

Focus does not mean single-mindedness.

❑ **Be Results-Oriented**

Focus on the outcome, not what you're going through.

CHAPTER 4

PERFORMANCE

Results Don't Lie

Excellence in execution is the only long-term competitive advantage.
—Raul Cesan, former president and chief operating officer,
Schering-Plough Corporation

As Jonathon and I were hiking in the Blue Ridge Mountains, he told me a wonderful story about a legendary monk in Zen lore named Joshu. This story came up as we walked high on the mountain trail and reflected on how incredible it was to have absolutely nothing else to do for the day but talk about the concept of performance. It was an extraordinary experience simply to give ourselves over to the luxury of time: to take a thought and think it all the way through without interruption.

Here is the tale of Joshu. A young monk was spending his first night in the monastery and was plagued with anxiety. All the other monks seemed so in the flow, experienced, and sure of themselves as they busied about their many tasks. Confused about what to do next, the novice approached Joshu, the senior student, to ask his help. "Have you had your dinner?" Joshu asked the novice. "Yes," the young monk replied. "Then go wash your bowl." It was in that simple answer at that moment that the young monk found himself beginning to enter into understanding about what was going on in the monastery. The message was that our job is simply to give each moment what is required: All that exists is the present moment. Be here now.

It got me to thinking. My position as chairman at Euro RSCG Life Becker was coming to an end. Joshu telling the young monk to wash his bowl was a story about someone discovering the simplicity of doing and finishing one thing at a time, doing it expertly and completely, and only then moving on to the next activity. As I reflected on fifteen years of work now in its end game, I considered the situation in Joshu's terms. I thought about all the tasks completed and problems solved in a decade and a half. I mentally walked around my office and looked at the walls. The company's best work was displayed there—the big ideas, the great campaigns, and the messages that moved our clients' products far beyond anyone's expectation. But you know what wasn't on the walls? *The letter from a client praising us for getting a mediocre deliverable in by deadline.* Am I being facetious? Sure! But sometimes it felt like we were fighting an uphill battle just to avoid that letter.

Have you noticed the easy domination of the nonessential? Attending to phone calls, e-mails, faxes, meetings, and the like has become much of our day. The value of "multitasking" has been drilled into us, and then we kid ourselves into believing that our creative inspiration is intact and not dispersed among the many details we tend to in the day. When we permit ourselves to pour our time into only the daily maintenance of office life, we become survivors but rarely true performers. Performance takes single-mindedness. To be able to truly perform on a field of excellence requires an incredible amount of concentration and focus. The really great (and important) work takes time and requires energy.

So Joshu teaches us a subtlety of leadership. It takes practice to learn the value of doing one thing at a time in a culture that asks us to do fifty; but the payoff is recovery of balance, excellence, and above all, focus. If your work life is out of focus you can't see anything. The mind is not an operating system with multiple programs running—the mind works best with one clear thought at a time. And if that thought is not given full attention it passes by undeveloped. Our business culture, with its attending technology mania, can easily dupe us into believing that the mind can be treated like another technology. But this is not the case. The mind is special and works best when we treat it as such.

Jon:

There is a saying in Zen: "A finger pointing to the moon." The finger represents the teaching and the moon is reality itself. Too often, the masters say, students mistake the finger for the moon. It is only by fully attending to one moment that the next one can show up unencumbered. Zen is a very simple practice, the masters say: When we eat we eat, when we sleep we sleep, and when we clean we clean. Developing yourself to be nimble enough to simply respond readily to the present as it unfolds is actually not as simple as it sounds . . . it is an unending practice.

FOCUS

Don't leave a task until you feel it's an A+ execution.

Like everybody else, a leader has limited time and energy, so choosing how to expend these precious commodities makes all the difference between performing exquisitely or just getting by. I have found that when you follow the goal of performing at an A+ level, certain extraneous tasks simply drop away on their own. And when that happens, it usually means they're not important enough to make the MOST IMPORTANT NOW priority list. Try saying "most important now" to yourself when the list is long, people are lined up outside your door, and the phone is ringing. Then the "delegate, delegate" music also comes on. Try thinking about exquisite execution as a life achievement. Over time, I have put together a short list of five focus to-dos that I have come to depend on throughout my career.

1. Never Leave a Task Until It's A+

Be an artist in everything and in even the little things you do. Your personal commitment to quality will earn you, your team, and your company credibility and profit over the long term. Realize that every task you put your individual stamp on is something that directly reflects on you—expressing your quality and nature. As my advertising colleagues and staff heard for fifteen years: "If it ain't great don't do it, don't fix it, don't present it." Only you know what your truly best work is; don't cheat yourself out of the reward of executing an A+ deliverable.

2. Redo the To-Do List Daily

Refocus your energy and make your performance new every day. Know the tasks in front of you and focus on what today is essential to make happen. Don't let a task sit on your list too long or it loses its vitalness. In rewriting your list, don't just copy it—rethink it. Process all tasks as if you have just seen them for the first time.

Think new solutions to old problems, more direct routes to answers. Focus yourself by asking, What would your competitor do?

3. Check Messages at Specified Times

E-mail, voice mail, faxes, snail mail, requests—set specific intervals in your day, or every other day, when you will attend to them. If you have a trusted someone else, let that person go through your messages and get rid of the junk mail and prioritize the rest. Keep true to your timing for go-through intervals. And then stop. If not, you will remain besieged by constant interruption. Focusing means one thing at a time and attending to it well.

4. Close Your Door

Just as you schedule time for others who want to meet with you or whom you want to meet, schedule time for you *with you*. Fully devote yourself to the project at hand. Put a "meeting in progress" sign on your door and go to work. If you allow yourself to be interrupted by a call or whatever when you are in the middle of thinking through a strategic problem, then both tasks get short shrift. You'll be amazed at the peace and productivity that comes from completely focused and uninterrupted work time.

5. Enjoy Your Work and Curb the Number of Meetings

Do good work. Truly engage in solving a problem, learn something new every day and strive to connect with others in an authentic way. It is almost impossible to perform well over the long term if you don't enjoy the work. Expect that performing well will give you joy. Great performers say that when they are in the flow of their activity they can actually feel time stop. Attain this flow as often as you can. It's the joy-juice of performance. By the way, how many extraneous meetings do you attend each week that take away valuable "focus" time? Find ways to limit them so they don't suck up your time.

Joshu, the Zen monk Jonathon and I talked about in the Blue Ridge Mountains, had it right. It's significant to your sense of well-being to do one thing at a time fully, with all of your concentration, and when finished, to go on to the next thing that same way. When that is your habit, every task takes on positive meaning. String days of meaning together and you're living a life of higher meaning. Not a bad life sentence.

ENTREPRENEURSHIP

Conduct your job as though it is your own *place of business.*

Raul Cesan, former president and COO of Schering-Plough, mastered the ability to remain entrepreneurial within the confines of a large organization. He encouraged every employee to run her territory or job as if it was her own personal business. It was his conclusion that when you run your own entrepreneurial business, going out of business is not an option. Cesan pressed his people to change the market and change the game in part, and he showed them how to do it when he rejected the company's first-year sales forecast of $500 million for allergy drug Claritin. He knew this groundbreaking drug could go further. What was his endgame and the message behind his turndown? "You compensate people when they grow the company." Raul Cesan is all about thinking big—big risk, big return. He energized his people incredibly by instilling this risk-welcoming behavior. It was Cesan—Mr. Performance—who again broke new ground by facilitating the Schering launch of the company's first major direct-to-consumer advertising campaign, again for Claritin. This initiative went on to help Claritin achieve an astounding 55 percent market share so that, subsequently, the product became a $3.5 billion brand—the first true blockbuster prescription drug.

So that is the short story of how a shift in performance expectations by Raul Cesan changed not only a single product launch, but also the shape of product launches and performance expectations to come for the entire pharmaceutical industry.

BENCHMARKING

All work must be measurable and measured.

Cesan told the Fordham Leadership Forum about seven principles. These principles were the benchmarks against which every action taken at Schering under his leadership was measured. Most will sound familiar by now.

1. A SENSE OF URGENCY—If you don't get things done in your business because it feels too hard, the competition will find a way to get it done.

2. FOCUS—Identify the critical goal, and do not be distracted from its execution.

3. INNOVATION—We must constantly find new and better ways to do business and outsmart the competition.

4. TEAMWORK—We must share our energy, our efforts, and our resources; forget about hierarchy—it is the successful conclusion we are after.

5. OPEN COMMUNICATION—We must make sure the benefits of teamwork flow smoothly among everyone by sharing ideas, insights, and experiences on a regular basis.

6. ACCOUNTABILITY—Every objective must be pursued with a sense of personal responsibility and ownership.

7. DECENTRALIZATION—Bureaucracy and paperwork must be kept to a minimum. The goal is to streamline the operation so we can lead the category.

Between Cesan's performance-culture management philosophy and Bill Toppeta's performance evaluation system (described next), we see two ways to encourage performance and measure the results of that encouragement. The message: Leadership is not just about ideas, but about implementation.

URGENCY

Do it before your competitors do.

For more than 100 years, MetLife was strictly a mutual insurance company (which is another way of saying it was slow and pokey). It went public just six years ago. When it made the shift from a mutual to a public company, MetLife's return on investment was only 7 percent. The competition was doing twice that. Bill Toppeta was up against tradition that fostered steady-state, "don't rock the boat" performance. Toppeta had evidence of the general complacency malaise. The year before MetLife went public, 86 percent of the company officers were ranked in performance as either "excellent" or "very good." It's no surprise, to impartial observers, that corporate performance did not correlate with the individual assessments. Toppeta knew he had to get the boat rocking. He had to get his people back to a place of "unknowing."

When Toppeta talked to his people about changing, he recognized it was more than likely that 86 percent of his managers weren't listening because they thought they were doing just fine. To rock the boat, the company put in place a new performance evaluation system that worked in two directions—vertical and horizontal. This is a great thing to adapt to your business, and many of my MBAs have.

It works like this: First, managers were asked to use a lifeboat ranking for their team. If there are thirty people on the manager's team, each person had a value rank from one to thirty. Second, each member of the team is evaluated on a scale of five down to one, in relation to everyone else in their strata (e.g., all group vice presidents are rated against each other, all the sales managers, etc.). Only 10 percent of the team can be assigned the highest rating of five; 20 percent are eligible to get rated four; 50 percent are eligible for a rating of three; and the remaining 20 percent can get rated either two or one. If you received a rating of one, you are gone. A ranking of two places you on probation. This is a system to see into the ranks and end the homogenization of the team. Good isn't good enough anymore.

While you'd think the adoption of this new system would create a cutthroat culture at MetLife, it didn't. As Toppeta pointed out: "In an organization of our size and a business of our complexity, it is far too complicated to accomplish almost anything by yourself. If you can't cooperate and get others to buy into your vision, you're not going to make it."

It comes back to Frances Hesselbein's assertion that "good leadership has a lot to do with good manners." Performance without perspective and principles is empty. It can easily turn into greed. If you need to make the quarter by distribution scams or phony restructuring accounting, it's bad news. Remember that it was Bill Toppeta who said that you can't measure the "why" of someone's performance, you can only measure the "what" and "how." When performance measurement is executed with precision, a leader can easily see if her people are achieving their goals in ways that promote collaboration with their team.

The best leaders model what they want their followers to perform. Bill Toppeta and Raul Cesan would not have been able to create such successful performance-based cultures on such a grand scale if they themselves did not model the performance they wanted. A leader must be both an incredible coach and a great player—certainly the hardest working player on the field.

INNOVATION

When the system isn't performing, change the system.

Might you think the formula for performance is much different in the much smaller nonprofit world? If you answered yes, you'd be wrong. Despite the difference in size, scale, and culture, performance is something that is pretty universal. As counterpoint to my tales of performance in major corporations, Jon introduced me to the work of an outstanding nonprofit performer in his region of the country. He had come into contact with this organization through his *Asheville Citizen-Times* column on Creativity at Work.

This organization, called HandMade in America, is an excellent model of performance. Based in Western North Carolina, Hand-Made in America is a ten-year-old private organization nationally recognized as one of the most innovative and successful nonprofits in the world. Rebecca (Becky) Anderson, who is economic developer, executive director, and HandMade's visionary, has been with the organization from the beginning.

Anderson undertook a huge challenge: to create a new system of economic development that she believed would work to overcome the region's losses in manufacturing and service jobs, year after year, to foreign competition. With help from Dan Ray, a long-term nonprofit and civic strategic planner, as well as others too numerous to mention, Anderson saw that Western North Carolina had to stop trying simply to import temporary jobs into the Blue Ridge region, but instead begin to cultivate the rich resources already at home.

Capitalizing on the abundant number of people working in the area in traditional arts and crafts and design, HandMade's philosophy was to sound the horns and celebrate this unusual conglomeration of artisan talent. HandMade built entrepreneurial networks of craftspeople across the region and additionally collaborated with colleges to help craftspeople with traditional skills obtain the best training—both in their craft and in business management. Anderson's exquisite performance far exceeded the expectations of all stakeholders, and subsequently resulted in HandMade being recognized in 2004 by *Worth* magazine as one of the top twenty-five arts nonprofits in the United States where you get "the biggest bang for your buck" and as being representative of the best in our country's culture. HandMade in America was the *smallest* nonprofit recognized alongside such entities as the Boston Symphony, The John F. Kennedy Center for the Performing Arts, New York's Metropolitan

Museum of Art, and Lincoln Center. It is a regional development organization that operates according to Raul Cesan's rules for the entrepreneurial organization; as a result, it has built a $200 million industry with hardly any bureaucracy or infrastructure.

Because of her success, Anderson now advises the top tourism officials in the Czech Republic and in South Africa, among others. Her approach stresses three questions that she developed and calls the key to HandMade's success: 1) Where are your sacred places in the community? 2) Where do you not want visitors? 3) How would you define your heritage, and which part of it would you want to share with tourists?

In asking these questions, Anderson turns talent, heritage, and beauty into the drivers of local economic development. Adapted, these three queries provide great performance insights for any business. And profitable answers.

Jonathon's Perspective

Don't waste life in doubts and fears.
Spend yourself on the work before you.
—RALPH WALDO EMERSON

The American philosopher John Dewey, best known for his theories on education, was one of the key founders of pragmatist philosophy, the truly American brand of theory that says something is of value only when it works in the real world and when it has "cash value." Dewey also said that if an idea does not have "cash value," it should be cast aside in favor of one that does. Dewey revolutionized a lot of people's thinking when he taught that ideas themselves do not have inherent value; only how those ideas perform in reality matters. Performance is that practice that either has "cash value" or not; it is easily measured.

For this reason, I think my generation can grasp onto the practices of this chapter quite well and adopt them as our own without much trouble. The one I want to specifically address here is focus, because without focus, everything else is diluted. Focus is the central ingredient of performance. It's like a packet of yeast to bread baking. It's looks almost insignificant, but without it, nothing happens—the bread doesn't rise.

I saw this focus in action when interviewing Chancellor John Bardo at Western Carolina University. I noticed a typed daily agenda sheet on his conference table. Box after box was filled next to each time slot. During the course of our interview, we ran over and his scheduler came in to alert the chancellor that a meeting was waiting for him. Bardo politely nodded to the scheduler without missing a beat in the conversation. As he came to the important point he wanted to make, the scheduler came in again, this time insisting the chancellor excuse himself. Without breaking concentration, Bardo finished his point just as he wanted to, stood up to shake my hand, and thanked me as though he had all the time in the world. Only then was he off.

And as rumor has it, this is how Bardo does everything, fully committed, never breaking focus. This noteworthy quality of his has translated into unprecedented performance for the university.

I found out that when he first arrived at the university, Bardo spent six months touring the state, visiting and listening to various constituencies. Bardo believes that "before you ever pronounce what you want to do, you better darn well listen to what people can handle." The thing he heard across the board from faculty, students, parents, and others was that they wanted graduates to obtain a top-notch, state-of-the-art education at home in Western North Carolina, and after graduation, they wanted to retain their local roots and be able to remain in the Blue Ridge Mountains. They wanted there to be a local economy to support them.

John Bardo makes it his business to try and deliver on what is asked of him. In his ten years at Western Carolina University, Bardo has been able to significantly raise academic standards, open a residential Honors College, put into play a national model Greek organization "plan for excellence," and create nine endowed professorships. WCU has also been designated a National Merit sponsoring university. The icing on the cake is that WCU has been able to conduct a $195 million university-wide rejuvenation, including a new fine arts and performing arts center, applied technology center, and center for the study of aging. Enrollment in 2004 rose to a number that wasn't predicted until 2012.

Bardo has the quality of staying true to what matters most. And while you might think that with that comes the "heavy weight of responsibility," what I experienced in John Bardo was a person enjoying himself, getting pleasure from not leaving a matter until it was well executed. In Bardo, I saw my father's point about the relationship between excellent performance and joy in the work. Distractions are everywhere in our culture, so much so that if we don't have them we tend to find a way to interrupt ourselves simply because we are so used to it; like checking e-mail in the midst of writing a report. To perform well I find I have to make myself dispense with those distractions that are soon forgotten after they are addressed. Performance is staying on that task that will define us as an "A+" performer.

If we don't do something heartfelt with our time at work, then we miss the best opportunity we will ever have to tangibly produce our values and character and put our will into action in the world outside our homes and immediate circle. Like artists, we too can imprint ourselves in our work. It took Auguste Rodin thirty-seven years to finish his masterpiece, the *Gates of Hell*—not very efficient.

But over that time period he perfected his craft, practiced new techniques, failed, returned to the work, and built a family of images that ultimately became separate masterpieces in their own right. Our next project at work may not be quite so encompassing, but nevertheless it can be a kind of gate for us. One that opens out to show the world a performance that is unmistakably ours.

PERFORMANCE

Checklist for Leaders

Practice/Activity

❏ Focus

Don't leave a task until you feel it's an A+ execution.

❏ Entrepreneurship

Conduct your job as though it is your *own* place of business.

❏ Benchmarking

All work must be measurable and measured.

❏ Urgency

Do it before your competitors do.

❏ Innovation

When the system isn't performing, change the system.

CHAPTER 5

PERSISTENCE

"No" Is Only for Today

Nothing in the world can take the place of persistence. Talent will not;
nothing is more common than unsuccessful men with talent. Genius will
not; unrewarded genius is almost a proverb. Education will not; the world is
full of educated derelicts. Persistence and determination alone are
omnipotent.—President Calvin Coolidge

The subject today was "persistence," and Jonathon wanted to hike
to a place a couple of hours from his house in Asheville called the
Cataloochee. We climbed up the trail by way of a valley that once
was home to more than 1,000 settlers who came to the mountains
of North Carolina from Scotland and Ireland to find a better life.
We walked in the footsteps of pioneers who made just about everything for themselves. So they could bake bread and feed their animals, they grew the wheat and corn in the fields and constructed
the waterwheel-powered mill for grinding that wheat and corn into
flour and meal. Not to be overlooked, they also made their own
clothes, candles, and tools. It's admirable and almost impossible to
fathom from my city point of view, where I'm lucky if I remember
to buy milk and pick up my dry cleaning. What was termed "sub-
sistence farming," we can aptly rename "persistence farming."

The hundreds of yards of stone walls that Jonathon led me by
as we hiked out of the valley and into the mountain on the "Little

Cataloochee Trail" have been standing here for more than 100 years. There is no mortar to hold the stones together, just careful placement with diligent hands. To construct these walls required an unbelievable amount of focus and quiet, unremitting attention; and as a result of the effort they still stand. Jonathon points out the almost perfect fit of the stones, like pieces of a jigsaw puzzle, each one made stronger by finding its home in the cleft of the other. Jonathon put his hand on a particularly odd-shaped moss-covered stone. "Imagine how many they had to throw back on the pile before they found this one?" he said. I smiled. It made me think of the work of those women and men I admire, and of all that is sacrificed in the pursuit of that perfect outcome—that moment when you know you have solved today's problem in the best possible manner.

A handmade wall of interlocking stones, a distinguished university or municipal police department, a great company—it always takes more than you thought you had. It always takes getting past your own personal limits for the sake of a goal greater than yourself.

I was running my hand across the stones, following Jon's as we walked, touching the moss and grass growing in between, when Jon asked me about my own story of persistence. He encouraged me to tell it because I use lots of examples of other people's lives in this book and he thought it only fair that I reveal my own. And so as we walked in a place of pioneer ventures so very different from my own, I told him.

MY OWN STORY

I've been a stutterer since I was five years old. When I started school, I had no trouble understanding what my teachers wanted, but I did have trouble answering their questions, because I stuttered badly back then. My stuttering got even more pronounced in grade school at the Yeshiva Torah Vodaath (a Jewish parochial school) I attended. My mother took me to every speech clinician she could find. They told her that she had to get me out of "that school" first and foremost. My father was dead set against my leaving the Yeshiva, but Mom told him unconditionally after sixth grade I wasn't going back. If he insisted, she would leave him. I enrolled in Public School 16. The stuttering lessened, but not completely.

I went on to Brooklyn's Boys High School, and by my junior year I was treasurer of the class, head of the Honor Society, and editor of the newspaper. In my senior year, as editor of the yearbook, I gave speeches. I was a baseball pitcher on an outstanding, racially mixed team. I worked on being out front all the time. I was constantly anxious about my stuttering, but at the same time, something was happening to me. Maybe it was how my mother brought me to speech therapy on two buses and a train. Or maybe it was how she taught herself to play baseball so she could teach me. Or maybe it was because I saw her teach herself how to play the piano. I can still hear her voice, "You can do *anything*, Sander!" I saw that she wasn't ever going to give up on me and that she was prepared to go absolutely all the way. I am convinced that this is ultimately the most important thing a person needs—total conviction that It Can Be Done.

A series of fortuitous circumstances brought me a walk-on potential baseball scholarship to Ohio State University. (I got cut after spring training.) Yet there I was, walking beside cornfields, the farthest thing from Brooklyn that I could imagine. I was in a new country, a pilgrim. A liberal arts education, studying, baseball, fraternity, girls, football, the marching band—there was no better place for me to be than Ohio State in the fifties. I owe a lot to that school.

After the army and some first jobs—one of which was as an "ethnic issues" speechwriter for Robert Kennedy during his 1964 Senate race—I went to work in the pharmaceutical industry, landing a job in public affairs at Lederle Laboratories, a division of American Cyanamid (now Wyeth). I went to school at night and on weekends to earn my MBA and I graduated in the top 5 percent of my class at Fairleigh Dickinson University. It wasn't because I was smartest; clearly I wasn't. I just worked harder and longer. My mom put a fire in me to be the absolute best at everything I was doing, and I have done my fair share to heap logs on that fire so that I could always be better tomorrow than I am today. As was the custom in the seventies at Fairleigh Dickinson, the top students of its MBA program were invited to join the adjunct faculty. Scared to death of having to stand up every week and speak to a large lecture hall, I did it anyway. I loved teaching and found it kept me a step ahead of my peers and often taught me more than I was expecting. I've kept it up to this day.

I worked at Lederle Laboratories for eighteen years. I launched or restaged over twenty products and worked on every aspect of marketing in the pharmaceutical business. I moved up the ladder, not as quickly as I wanted, but still I moved. As I approached the VP of marketing spot, I kept getting passed over. I worked harder and harder still. Finally, I was passed over yet again for a job that many of my colleagues thought should have been mine. I wasn't given an explanation. Disheartened and disillusioned with a company that I had put my blood, sweat, and soul into, I accepted my first call from an executive recruiter. It was an advertising agency in New York City. I said farewell to Lederle.

One day years later, I got a call from one of the senior people at Lederle inviting me to lunch. He had been my boss, so I agreed to meet him, out of respect. It was Christmas Eve that year and cold in Nanuet, New York. I sat down at the table and don't remember chitchatting, though I'm sure we did. I remember him leaning in while he confided, "Sander, I asked you here to tell you I have prostate cancer and the prognosis is not good. There's something I need you to know. You got passed over for the big job because someone on the Lederle executive committee thought that stuttering was a sign of mental illness. He thought you'd be an embarrassment to the company. Nobody had the courage to overrule him. I should have." I felt someone had just whacked me across the chest with a sledgehammer.

I remember walking outside into the bitter cold, literally shaking and in a bit of a fog. But I got past it. As the snow fell so did the memory—just gone. It didn't matter anymore. I was glad my old boss could relieve his conscience, and gladder still that the sorry story was less about me and more about him. I looked back at the restaurant, its name, Hong Luck, lettered above the roof, and I laughed. I had just been told something really crappy, something that if I had known years before would have boiled my blood right out of my veins. But now, in that moment, I felt only how lucky I was. Lucky that I knew the secret was to persist despite the circumstances.

The point isn't that we've had hard times; the point is what we do with them. Do we turn them into excuses or challenges? It's been more than nineteen years since that Christmas Eve night at Hong Luck in Nanuet, and looking back now, I realize how much that experience has served me. How it propelled me to become an advocate for stutterers and never to ever allow some backward notion of stuttering to place a stigma on somebody.

After some stops and starts, I found myself at a new home. I was named CEO of Robert A. Becker, a venerable healthcare advertising agency. The agency was on a "downtrend" and its English (now French) owners wanted me to turn things around. Neither the recruiter nor I had been told that this innocuous-sounding downtrend meant Becker was about to lose its three biggest clients. Merck, Pfizer, and Sandoz (now Novartis) were about to walk away. By the time I came on board, they were gone—and so was 60 percent of Becker's income. Down to thirty people, with only one substantial piece of business left, things looked grim. I tried to look on the bright side. We were so far down already, no one would ever know if I failed to turn things around. Happily we did.

I firmly believe that persistence separates the great ones from the mediocre. Persistence is the ability to see difficulty simply as territory through which you have to navigate. It's easy to be deterred by difficult circumstances—it's easy to find any excuse to quit. "Quitting" is not part of the vocabulary; it's not an option. To practice persistence, leaders have to train themselves to shun rejection—no matter how hurtful—to take a lot of deep breaths and to have eyes trained to spot the next opportunity to win. And most important, leaders must be willing to work beyond any notion of personal limitation until the job, whatever that takes, is done. True leaders do not excuse themselves or lay blame on others for their difficulty. They do not add to a situation the extra burden of their displeasure with the difficulty at hand; they evaluate the course for what it is and take action.

The Fordham Leadership Forum guest speakers agree that persistence is the ability to drive relentlessly and resourcefully toward the accomplishment of a desired end and to do it regardless of external circumstances. The mantra I apply in my company is:

NO IS ONLY FOR TODAY; FIGHT FOR A YES TOMORROW. FIGHT UNTIL YOU GET IT!

TRANSCEND LIMITS

Whatever beliefs you're carrying around about your limitations—let them go—move past them.

The quote by Calvin Coolidge on persistence that starts off this chapter has been hung on the wall in I don't know how many executive offices. It is advice that's easy to frame and hang, quite another to practice. Jon and I have spent time turning over ideas about Forum leader Howard Safir, whose career epitomizes Coolidge's words. When you ask Safir how he did it, he'll tell you it was through iron-willed persistence. "I volunteered for every single thing that anybody didn't want. If somebody had an assignment that was long, [or] meant you needed to work nights, weekends, [or] it wasn't very interesting, I volunteered for it." The reason he always volunteered is because of his belief that you cannot have an effect if you're not in the game. "You have to be willing to do whatever it takes and win at it," he told us. Whatever it takes, a leader has to be willing to do it (time and again) if she is going to succeed.

A couple of my students probed Safir; they wanted to know if the kind of persistence he demonstrated as such a young person was attributable to his unbelievable amount of confidence. Did he think it was something you were born with, they wanted to know. He thought a minute and said, "Maybe it just takes a desire to do the right thing no matter what, and the confidence comes later."

A statement like that, made in an unscripted way, can silence a room—and it did. Truth is, everyone's scared at first. Especially when you're young and have an idea burning inside you, and the boss asks if anyone has anything to add. What if you know in your gut that you're right, but saying so will put you in contradiction of the boss's idea, or society's? What do you do? It's not confidence at that point that forces you to speak. It's the notion that if you're going to look yourself in the mirror the next day and the day after that, you have to say what you think.

Ideas, not ego, drive persistence. And that's how you firm up your leadership skills for the long haul—now you make a believer out of yourself. And when you yourself start to believe, it will begin to show and others will believe, too.

Faith Popcorn told us that she had to practice looking in the eye of critics who said her ideas about consumers were all wrong. And as she tells it, it was lonely out there:

> "No one in the late eighties was focusing on the female consumer, or the return of nostalgia, or the pent-up desire to get out of the clubs and under the covers cocooning with a pizza. When we told the [management of] Sheraton Hotels to start thinking about accommodating their Las Vegas hotels for families, they actually laughed. When I told The Coca-Cola Company that water was going to be the young consumer's drink of choice and to put a water lever on the 'home fountain,' you could have sold my stock for two cents in their eyes. But I persisted and we made it through. It wasn't ego. I knew my methodology worked. It's part of my job to get my clients to see ahead and not back down from what they see. It's a natural thing to want to shoot the messenger, especially if you have to turn around your big Titanic of a company before it sinks. Persistence to me is having the guts to keep at what you know is right. But I will say this, you never really get used to being the only voice in the wilderness."

Persistence as a quality isn't inborn; it is the circumstances of life that force it out. Like Howard Safir said, when those circumstances show themselves, you have to be ready to get in the game immediately—to stand up and be counted. Persistence is a kind of stubborn prickliness—a sense that you're not willing to rest until things are made right.

And it's important to realize that lots of leaders don't go around looking for the job. The job frequently finds them because their ideals and general sense of what's right gets noticed and often takes them there.

Randy Thurman, CEO of VIASYS Healthcare, told me that he thinks people become leaders when they are placed in a specific situation where those traits can emerge. Without that situation, one where you have to struggle to accomplish what needs to be done, persistence may never be tested.

FOCUS RELENTLESSLY ON A POSITIVE OUTCOME

Difficulties and challenges are a part of life.
Be relentless; get to the solution through a strong focus.

Thomas Von Essen, the New York City fire commissioner during 9/11, is a great example of someone who had to learn how to move on boldly if he was to survive. Disarmingly honest, Von Essen is quick to tell you that he flunked out of college the first time around and quick to tell you that he became a firefighter because he didn't know what else to do; he needed a job and thought he could handle the physical aspects of the work.

What he doesn't tell you is that he finished college and graduate school while he was with the NYC Fire Department, that he led the firefighters union in a more open and constructive way than it had ever been run before, and that for six years preceding the tragedy of 9/11, he quietly brought tremendous innovation to his role as fire commissioner. He won't tell you all that, but it's all in the record and other people will tell you. Persistence is written all over him.

He told the Leadership Forum class that after 9/11, it was all about getting up every day, putting one foot in front of the other, and doing the best you could—it was about persistence, plain and simple. In his words:

> "What was I supposed to do? Quit? I took to joking around to take the edge off things to keep my head together. And the mayor said to me, 'I never realized you were so funny.' I said to him, 'Well, I never wanted to fool around with you before, 'cause I thought you'd fire me. Now, you couldn't get anybody to take this job, so there's really no sense in me holding back.' The mayor laughed his head off at that. Everybody wanted to be fire commissioner before September 11. But, when 9/11 hit, there wasn't anybody applying for that job. So, you have to just grab yourself and say, these are the people I spent thirty-two years with, and you just keep going."

If you are (or want to be) a leader, like Von Essen, you keep going. That's why the nine Ps of leadership, as covered in this book, are practices and not pronouncements. It has to be a code of belief, a daily effort. Like the Dalai Lama teaches and Jon often references, everyone is given this incredible opportunity to build the most important legacy you have—your own life. And more often than not, it's persistence that is the dividing line between a good intention and a good deed. Anyone can have good intentions, but persistence gets the job done for all the stakeholders and will earn the respect of your peers and your own self.

Arthur Hiller, senior vice president of Millennium Pharmaceuticals, is one of the most innovative leaders in the rapidly developing blended industries of biotechnology, pharmaceuticals, and genomics. His industry moves at an accelerated pace, so Hiller fo-

> ## *Jon:*
>
> *The Dalai Lama said, "Live a good, honorable life. Then when you get older and think back, you'll be able to enjoy it a second time." Doing the right thing in the moment has its payoff in the long term. Memory can be a joy or a torment, and the choices we make today determine how we build this human mechanism of comfort or derision. It is only in practicing persistence that we truly learn to respect and value our character; but those things that are tough for us, when we do them anyway, we never forget it.*

cused the class on the necessity to have the courage to greet failure and persist, not to fear starting anew when the tack you've taken is met with adversity.

During his presentation, Hiller put up a slide and went on to tell the Forum students about a gentleman by the name of Charles Swindoll. He wrote a book called *Inspiration for Living,* and he hosts a daily radio show. Swindoll has a compelling view of persistence that Hiller has come to embrace and which bears repeating:

> The longer I live, the more I realize the impact of attitude on life. Attitude, to me, is more important than facts. It is more important than the past, than education, than money, than what other people think or say or do. It is more important than appearance, giftedness, or skill. It will make or break a company . . . a church . . . a home. The remarkable thing is, we have a choice every day regarding the attitude we will embrace for that day. We cannot change our past . . . we cannot change the fact that people

will act in a certain way. We cannot change the inevitable. The only thing we can do is play on the one string we have, and that is our attitude.

Persistency appears so simple, but it's incredibly difficult to execute. Like Hiller says, the most important activity in any given situation is what's happening inside your own head. Nobody but you controls whether you give up and quit. Chances are you will lose today, but there is always tomorrow or next week or next month. If you are willing to tolerate the discomfort and pain of rejection, the fear, loss, loneliness, whatever it is that habitually has pushed your buttons hard enough to make you stop trying, there is always another possibility. The first time your head is telling you to quit and you don't will be the hardest. But if you can push through that and then do it again (and again), you begin to create a new habit, a new history, and a new story of yourself. One of the keys is to start small.

I look to John Glenn whenever I start feeling that I can't take on the next challenge. When he wanted to return to space at age 77, most people thought he was joking, but he pressed on. He had created a habit of persistence for his entire life and broke through the age barrier, just as he had broken the sound barrier, because of his unwillingness to take "no" for an answer. He had to deal with people telling him that he couldn't do it at every turn—the media, NASA, his friends, his Senate colleagues, his family, and just about every comedian from New York to Los Angeles who took the opportunity to play up to the cultural affinity for ageism. But Glenn broke through it all and blasted off into space for the second time!

But this is John Glenn, Jonathon reminded me—white male, impeccable Marine Corps record, test pilot extraordinaire, former astronaut, senator, consummate and understated American hero. If anyone could do it, he could. Jonathon brought this point up as we hiked along the Cataloochee trail. And though I argued with him (there's a fine line between being stubborn and being persistent, you know), I finally had to admit the validity of the wider scope of what he was implying. Beyond the sound barrier and age barrier, I don't think there has ever been a bigger barrier to upper management ranks in the for-profit or nonprofit world than the color barrier.

This brings me to the story of one of my former MBA students, Sola Winley, who Jonathon had a long conversation with and who is well on his way to becoming an exceptional leader.

STRUGGLE FOR EXCELLENCE

"Good enough" is easy and beatable.
Never leave a job until you grade it A+.

At thirty-four, Winley had a master's degree in sports marketing, an MBA, and a master of social work (MSW) degree. He's unbelievably motivated. As an African-American male who grew up in a single-parent family, Winley had the cards stacked against him, but he didn't let circumstance get in his way. I met him during a very interesting transition in his life. He had worked in marketing for the National Football League for seven years. He was doing well, getting promoted, and making big dough. Then 9/11 hit and his world, like the rest of ours, turned upside down. He decided he wanted to do something of more meaning and substance, so he began to look at the nonprofit world.

But before we get into that, let me tell you a quick side story about Winley to help shed a little light on how we started to become friends, not just teacher and student. He took my class and I gave him a B+. He sent me an e-mail that read like a legal brief explaining why this grade was unacceptable to him. He outlined his course performance in detail. He made a lot of sense. I replied, challenging him to do additional work if he was serious about changing his grade. He had the extra work to me in a week, and it was some of the most impressive material a student has ever shown me. He earned his A. When Winley graduated (at the top of his class), he gave me a book that I keep close at hand. It was the sayings of the Greek philosopher Epictetus, and he underlined this quote: *"Practice yourself, for heaven's sake, in little things; and thence proceed to greater."* Sola Winley was indeed going on to great things. And he taught me a lot about what persistence was all about and why he wanted every class to be his best class.

After a long soul search, Winley discovered St. Christopher's, Inc.—a social work program with wraparound services whose focus is keeping families together. In business in New York since 1881, it sponsors medical services, day care, job training, parenting classes—you name the family need and St. Christopher's did it. Amazingly, even the CEO of St. Christopher's tried to talk Winley out of leaving his corporate job. Winley persisted, took a huge pay cut, and went to work.

The CEO of St. Christopher's made Winley a proposition. He asked Winley if he wanted to create something from the ground up. To that challenge, Winley said yes, and what he conjured up was the Institute for Leadership and Change, an executive development institute for managers of color in the nonprofit arena. Winley says he was in the right place at the right time, but when you hear the details, Jon and I see it that Winley created the place through sheer persistence. In only two years, he built the institute from idea to functioning program. He was given the freedom to create the structure, the business plan, the mission, and the vision. He did it all and it worked.

The Institute for Leadership and Change takes on fifteen non-profit executives at a time and works with them for ten weeks. The participants are mostly African-American and Latino, and 40 percent of them are women. Winley was able to obtain the meeting space for the institute within the Merrill Lynch headquarters. He did this to make a practical as well as a symbolic point. "When we meet in a building where the chief executive of the largest financial institution in the world is African-American, this has an impact. We may not talk about it all the time, but we know it's there. If Stanley O'Neal could get to the top of his organization, then our participants can surely make it to executive director of their non-profits one day—that's the message," says Winley.

The Institute for Leadership and Change makes it a point to be up-front about the facts that impede leaders of color from rising through the ranks, while being insistent that current circumstances do not equal future outcomes. Winley and his group also deal head on with the common finding that for executives of color, the rules are different when it comes to being promoted. Says Winley, "Risks are not traditionally taken on people of color; those risks are taken on people that upper management feels more comfortable with. To get to positions of power in organizations, people of color have to stay at their positions much longer, need to have a diverse group of wide ranging mentors, and must perform at 110 percent effort, 100 percent of the time."

Winley intimately knows that to overturn stereotypes you must practice persistence. His audience is a motivated group. His institute challenges them to go even deeper into their persistence reservoir, asking those who go through the training to look at the issue of color and its political and economic implications from every angle. This is done so the issue is not ignored or ignited, but rather dealt with realistically for what it is. Winley believes that "leadership is colorless—and that's the place we all have to get to—seeing a leader for his or her skills and character only." The Institute for Leadership and Change trains leaders of color to develop and nurture their desire to be the best at what they do—to make them so good that not promoting them would be an outrage.

Frances Hesselbein is on common ground with Sola Winley. As chairperson of the Leader to Leader Institute, founded by the guru of management practice, Peter F. Drucker, she is often asked to share her expertise regarding leadership and gender. Hesselbein is a leadership connoisseur; she has seen leadership evolve and grow as a business concern over her many years in the leadership industry. Like Drucker, who she says urges us to "focus on task, not on gender," her strongly held belief is that leadership is "genderless." Add to that Winley's conviction that it is "colorless" and we're getting to a new definition of a leader, where a leader can be any individual who applies himself to becoming and remaining one. Here's Hesselbein writing in her Fall 1999 *Leader to Leader* article, "Focus on the Task":

> Diversity of gender, race, culture, and background in our leadership teams strengthens and enriches our organizations. But that is not the reason we, as leaders who are women, do what we do. The mission that defines why we do what we do has no gender.

Talking to Hesselbein is like going to the Oracle of Delphi. You feel totally heard. She challenges you to maintain persistent attention in improving your leadership practice.

PERSEVERE

Winning can become a habit just like failure can.
Envision yourself succeeding. Make it happen.

Jeff Rich is the forty-three-year-old dynamic CEO of the NYSE-listed company ACS, which provides business process outsourcing

(BPO) to everyone from GE to the Social Security Administration. Keep in mind that Rich has been at the helm of ACS since he was twenty-nine; he built the company up from zero to $4 billion in revenue in just fourteen years. He told us a memorable story of how he learned to ask himself the right questions, and how he learned persistence was the way to gain success. Jonathon likes this one because it happened in a philosophy class.

When Rich was a freshman at the University of Michigan, his philosophy professor walked into class on the first day and set down a large beaker on his desk, followed by a bag. He then reached into the bag and pulled out some rocks. He filled the beaker up with rocks that were about half the size of a fist. And then he asked the class if they thought the beaker was full. Most of them said it was. The professor then reached under his desk and pulled out another bag and, opening it, started dumping handfuls of gravel into the beaker. Again, he filled it right up to the top. He asked the class again if they thought it was full. And, you know, a few people said, it looks full. The students were starting to get amused and wondered what this professor was up to. He pulled out another bag that he had stashed under the desk, this time one filled with sand. Then he removed a little scooper from his suit jacket and started pouring sand into the beaker. He packed it down like a mud pie and asked the question again. No one dared to answer this time. Then he grabbed a pitcher and poured a little bit of water into the beaker that the sand absorbed. Again he asked the class his question, but this time he answered it himself. "Okay. Now it's full! Now tell me why I did this?"

Rich recalled that there was a kid in the front row, a straight A student, at the ready with an answer to every question, usually without even considering it, so good was his photographic memory. He raised his hand. This kid's interpretation was that no matter how busy you get, if you organize properly, you can always fit more in. Hearing this, the philosophy professor shouted an emphatic "No," silencing the room. Rich, who was sitting in the back of the class, nearly nodding off, jumped when the professor shouted. As he was awakened, this is what he heard: The point of the professor's little demonstration was that if you don't put the big rocks in first, you'll never get them in. That answer woke Rich up in a permanent way, and today he uses this metaphor all the time with his own employees—"Remember the big rocks first."

And as Rich told the Fordham MBA students, "If you know what your big rocks are and keep them in focus, giving up is not an option—persistence is ultimately about loving something so much that you refuse to ever abandon it."

Bill Shore, the founder of Share Our Strength, also talked about persistence:

"It was at the same time that several enormously high profile hunger relief efforts were starting. They dwarfed us. Live Aid, U.S.A. for Africa, all the rock concerts, Hands Across America—there were all of these highly visible activities going on and we looked like a very marginal influence at the time. But what we said to ourselves was these other activities are great, but they're not going to be here in five years and we will. And that turned out to be true. So in some ways, those high-profile, short-term activities helped us to create our competitive advantage. Here was Live Aid raising tens of millions of dollars, and here we were in our first year raising only $30,000. It is very easy to ask yourself, and I did, why should we even do this? But we realized that we had an answer for the underlying problems of hunger and could become a long-haul persistent organization that would not go away until the problem went away. Seeing the high-profile nature of flash-in-the-pan organizations made the work ahead of us very clear. We had to do this work of ending world hunger day after day—long after the media wanted to move on to the next story. We knew that our job wasn't just to ameliorate, but to solve—to end world hunger—not just feed people. And you have to be prepared to hang around a long time if you want to do that.

"I encourage young people to drive right to it. I don't think you need to go out and get your ticket punched at all the stops. Find your thing and go for it—that's how success happens— because you care so much and want it so badly that you can't see yourself doing anything else but winning."

LOOK TO THE FUTURE, BUT LIVE IN THE PRESENT

Learn from the past. Focus on the present.
Plan for the future. Don't quit.

When "common sense" says you're crazy, you're on the right track. When someone tells you the goal is unreachable, when you have to face the fact that someone just will not and might never return your call, just smile on the inside and get to work! Think of space flight or the mapping of the human genome. Or better yet, think of the peace process in the Middle East and what you can do to help solve it. Such a future-focused thought is exactly what bred the unlikely business partnership between Hisham Jabi, a Palestinian man who grew up in the West Bank; Uri Pomerantz, a Drucker MBA graduate and an Israeli-American; and Bryan Berkett, an American Jew. Their slogan is "justice through pragmatism" and their microfinance company is Jozoor, Ltd.

The word *jozoor* means "roots" in Arabic, and it is this threesome's hope that their business idea gets at the root of the problems in the Middle East. In 2003, Pomerantz's aunt was killed on a busy Jerusalem street by a terrorist's bullet. A stray Israeli bullet killed Jabi's cousin while she sat nursing her eleven-day-old baby on her balcony. Berkett's grandparents are Holocaust survivors. Suffering is a common thread, not an excuse to quit. It is a catalyst that pushes them on toward peace and reconciliation, their ultimate goal.

> ## Jon:
>
> *I lived in the Old City of Jerusalem during the winter and spring of 1996. A little while after my return to the States, I wrote my most widely produced play,* Jerusalem Son. *The play is about an Israeli soldier who has a child with a Palestinian teacher and has to tell his nationalist Holocaust survivor parents about it. The play does not end happily. No character in the play is willing to persist to move beyond their entrenched ideas of self-righteous indignation. To me, this story that my dad cites here, about Jozoor microfinance, is what is most hopeful about ethical business practice. If these young, recent MBA grads can do it in Israel, it can be done anywhere. They demonstrate an incredible lesson for us: that the way to peace is through pushing away our greatest fears to achieve our greatest hopes with the persistence of a warrior.*

These men, scarred by crucible experiences, are driving straight toward what they want without regard for a time line for success. Back in my days, we all thought we had to "pay our dues" before we did anything we cared about. "You have to do well before you could do good' was a maxim of my generation. Generation X doesn't seem to have that kind of patience and hierarchical mindset (thank goodness).

Jozoor won the Stanford University Social Venture Business Plan competition in May 2003. The idea behind Jozoor was to supply small loans to rural Palestinian men between the ages of twenty and twenty-nine as a pragmatic alternative to terror. The initial test run was to finance fifty loans of $800 each, which means a lot in a region where 60 percent of the people live in poverty and exist on about $2 a day. Here's one case where it has worked. One of Jozoor's clients was a Palestinian man who grew cucumbers. With the almost daily attacks, increased security, and additional checkpoints, the man's cucumbers kept rotting before he could get them to market. Jozoor loaned the man the money he needed to turn his cucumber crop into a pickle business. Now he can more easily transport his aged cucumbers to market and keep his stock in good shape to sell. Despite the daily hardships, the man's business is doing well and he sees hope.

It is an interesting coincidence to me that all his life my own father also sold pickles. His particular pickles came out of a barrel standing on a wood floor in the appetizing store that bears our name in Williamsburg, Brooklyn, and still stands as it did ninety years ago. Am I connected to that Palestinian man? Of course I am. The grit of persistence knows no borders or barriers. One of the greatest jazz pianists of all time, Duke Ellington, said that a goal is a dream with an ending. With persistence, we don't just dream, we use every ounce of energy we have to get to the end of what we want accomplished. Even if that end takes us beyond our own lifetime, still we march forward step after step.

Jonathon's Perspective

The best way out is always through.
—ROBERT FROST

The first house Tami and I bought was a 900-square-foot box with the outside walls built entirely of cinderblock. The charm of it for us was that the front facade was covered in river stone. There was something about stone. When a commercial lot was being cleared not too far from my house, I made a deal with the developer that I could come by after hours and remove any stone I could lift myself. Over the course of a spring and summer, I picked the place clean and must have carted off nearly ten tons of gray, brown, red, and rust-colored stones in the back of my truck. Back at our place, I washed the stones and then went to figuring how I would integrate their character into our unevenly shaped yard and also tie into the stone facade of our house. I am not a methodical person. I work primarily by intuition. I was simply going to use what I had found, intent on finding a niche for every single stone that I had carted. I wound up building a stone fire pit, six stone benches to go around it, a stone Zen garden, a stone stream, a stone bridge, another very large stone bench in front of the Zen garden, stone steps, a stone walkway, a stone patio, and stone borders for all the flower beds we had created.

At the end of two years, I had touched every stone in my yard many times. I had built a world—or more accurately, a world had built itself. The shapes of the stones themselves determined their best place to fit the landscape. The stones made me bend to their will, not the other way around. This is a different way to look at persistence.

When Dad and I were walking on the Cataloochee trail and he was admiring the time and energy required to build the stacked stone walls, he was hitting on something that obviously resonated very deeply for me. Because of their distinctive shape, color, and weight, stones have their own sense of where they should be placed—the key is having the persistence to listen to them—to not resist their will. In the end, we do not build projects; projects build us, leaving indelible marks on our character.

And I guess this is an important distinction in how I see persistence in leadership. Western tradition says that the road to hell is paved with good intentions, but the Eastern tradition says that our intentions are all we have to go on. I fall in the Eastern camp. I do not believe that the individual is powerful enough on her own to affect the outcome she wants to see in any given situation. I learned a lot about this from the heavy rocks I got tired of moving around. I had a large load of rocks one weekend and I had every intention of making stone steps out of them. But as much as I wanted to, something about their sizes and shapes just wouldn't dig well into an incline. Exhausted and sweaty, I finally realized I was trying to make a stone stairway out of rocks clearly meant for a stone walkway. When I was able to get myself out of the way, the stones found their home and I had a new walkway and new insight—I would have to wait on the steps until the right stones showed up. This and countless other experiences taught me that although my intention is clear, I cannot always control the outcome. And if I could, life would not be nearly as interesting.

Persistence to me is not giving up, despite unpredictability. It is being able to accept that you need a walkway when your original intention was a staircase. In the end, you still have something that takes you somewhere, and you have the added realization that you had to bend and flex and acknowledge external circumstances to get you there. I very much concur with Arthur Hiller's emphasis on the importance of attitude, and I am in agreement with the quote from Charles Swindoll that he shared with us. In my view, persistence in leadership is not a fixed wrecking ball bearing down on a problem; it's more like a flexible high-tech instrument that has the ability to constantly recalibrate the external circumstances and make adjustments without prejudice or rancor on the way to a positive solution. Leaders such as Arthur Hiller are living proof that mastering the practice of persistence is the bare-bones price of entry to leadership.

When Howard Safir speaks of "whatever it takes," it makes absolute sense to baby boomers, because they did make those sorts of sacrifices to achieve the success they did—they had to. For them, it was not only important that they work hard and long, but that they were observed doing it—visibility. The boss had to see them at work early and staying late. Generation Xers saw the personal realities of this attitude and the toll it took on their parents (e.g., high divorce rates, high stress, early exits to new careers), and they said it's not worth it.

For my generation, work is not a portal to a paycheck; it has to be chock-full of moments that encourage us to express ourselves. Gen Xers measure success not by how long they work but by other valued measures such as: Do they enjoy work? Are they fairly compensated for the time they put in? Do they have the time they need to be who they are outside the job? This is unfamiliar territory to a lot of boomer businesspeople. It's not the way they came up the ranks. You even see publications featuring in-depth articles explaining how Gen Xers want job security but place a higher value on personal values than work goals. Time is sacred for Gen Xers; we know we can never get it back once we give it up.

Cam Marston, a workplace generational expert out of Charlotte, North Carolina, told me that "the previous generations measured performance often on hours spent working. You were a hard worker if you worked fifty-five to sixty hours a week. Xers and Millennials look at it differently. They look at what they get done in their time on the job. Their attitude is, my work is *not* my life. So they measure work more in terms of completion of projects than in hours."

So how do the generations work together effectively when their attitudes about persistence are so different? For many boomers and traditionals, they look at Gen X attitudes about the workplace and are taking a page out of their own book later in life. Noting the cost of sacrificing so much of their personal lives for their jobs, they are reshuffling many of their priorities, including how they define persistence.

Others feel that they paid their dues the hard way and so should the generations coming up behind them—"whatever it takes." I see a balance to be struck here.

If we can see that neither attitude is simply right or wrong, but rather that each is shaped by circumstantial realities, then together we can focus on what we really want in the workplace. Mine is an incredibly persistent generation in the sense that we are relentless in trying to find those work arenas where our most meaningful work can be accessed and appreciated. (Of course, Generation Xers have this luxury to be picky about personal time and personal values because their critical mass is so much less than that of the boomers. Competition with each other for the best jobs is not nearly as brutal.) But to the employer who can provide such a work environment, deservedly, loyalty is the reward.

What about Sola Winley's sense that leadership is colorless and Frances Hesselbein's belief that it is genderless? These sentiments resonate so loudly because the issues of racism and sexism are not glossed over as beside the point, but are dealt with and explored thoroughly. This is the greatest strength of persistence—to look right at limits with all of their ugly realities and then to become determined to walk right through them. To know that arcane paternalistic and ethnocentric notions about leadership are simply bogus, outdated stereotypes is crucial to the process—but knowing is not enough. To bring this message to the light of day and make it the norm requires all the persistence one has when one recalls the history we have inherited.

PERSISTENCE

Checklist for Leaders

Practice/Activity

❑ **Transcend Limits**
Whatever beliefs you're carrying around about your limitations—let them go—move past them.

❑ **Focus Relentlessly on a Positive Outcome**
Difficulties and challenges are a part of life. Be relentless; get to the solution through a strong focus.

❑ **Struggle for Excellence**
"Good enough" is easy and beatable. Never leave a job until you grade it A + .

❑ **Persevere**
Winning can become a habit just like failure can. Envision yourself succeeding. Make it happen.

❑ **Look to the Future, but Live in the Present**
Learn from the past. Focus on the present. Plan for the future. Don't quit.

CHAPTER 6

PERSPECTIVE

The Seeing Is in the Doing

You can't do anything by yourself, anything of any
significance, in my opinion.
—THOMAS VON ESSEN, NYC FIRE COMMISSIONER ON 9/11

Jon and I had decided to talk about the P of perspective while hiking Bear Mountain in upstate New York. Speaking for myself, I lacked in the area of perspective a lot when I was younger. Back then, I had to win every battle. I didn't make much distinction between the important ones and the petty ones. That's changed some now—for the most part. Age helps. My wife Mechele helps. She encourages me to take the long view and to laugh at the worst-case scenarios I tend to dream up.

On this hike up Bear Mountain, I want to talk more about Tom Von Essen, who was New York City's fire commissioner when the World Trade Center was attacked in 2001. When Von Essen came to speak to the Fordham Leadership Forum, he knocked the class out; I still hear from my students that that night was a life changer for them.

When a New York City veteran firefighter of thirty-two years, who helped get the city through the worst civilian disaster in the nation's history, talks to you, you listen hard. The thing about Von Essen is that he didn't need to use any leadership parables. He was, and his people were, literally tested by fire. Not for big bucks or accolades, but simply because it was the nature of the job. No sports metaphor or battle hyperbole needed—the leadership job he did is enough to inspire awe without dressing it up.

In the class, his forthrightness and self-deprecating humor had the effect of compelling my students into a state of reflection. Everyone took a hard look at themselves and their lives. That night it was embodied in front of all of us—great leadership is born of unceasing commitment. There is no amount of salary that can make someone a great leader. The motivation comes from within, from the deepest and most indescribable place.

One of my top students was visibly moved by Von Essen's presence; it seemed to bring the horrors of 9/11 right back for her. She wanted to hear a piece of truth from someone who lived through fire. But Von Essen cut right through any awe or sentimentality: "I don't know the reasons why some people deliver and some people don't. I don't know if it comes from the grammar school teachers you had, the times that you got beat up, or beat somebody up, when you were in the fifth grade. I don't know." He refused the pedestal.

Another of my students pressed him further on how anyone was able to make it through the post-event horror. He responded as plainly as if he were talking about the rain. "It didn't do the families any good to talk about some of the stuff that was going on. So you eat all that, and you kept it to yourself. Some of that is the worst part, not being able to tell people things." The students left that night feeling differently about leadership. They realized it was one of the hardest things in the world to do.

ACTIVITY

The ultimate reward of leadership is the activity itself.

Time has passed, but the feeling of that night has not. There is nothing outright "glorious" about leading. At its most basic, it is about accountability and service and taking a long view, and reflection. To do it well is hard, plain and simple. And when the chips are down, know that your character will be tested. To take on a position of leadership is not an activity to enter into lightly. Von Essen was instructive about the gravity that is involved when one takes on the role.

About a year after Von Essen spoke to the Forum, I read a book excerpt in the May 24, 2004, issue of the *Financial Times*. Taken from *Wisdom for a Young CEO* by Doug Barry, an adolescent from Philadelphia, it's a compendium of the 100 letters he wrote to the world's top CEOs and their responses.

Doug Barry didn't write me to seek advice about the road to becoming CEO; even if he had, I couldn't have offered him a formula to sum it up once and for all. My advice to him, and to all would-be leaders, is to find that thing you feel connected to and called to do. Leadership sometimes becomes a choiceless choice because your level of commitment qualifies you to inspire and teach others to build on your mission. But this is not an easy life that comes with a handbook for success. This life is one of rewarding struggle.

And if Barry cares about something this much, it will inevitably hurt. It will hurt when he can't succeed every day. It will hurt when he is working long hours and gets home after his children have gone to bed. So quite simply, if you don't absolutely have to lead, I would tell Barry not to set out to do it. The money and title aren't worth it; there are more important things in life. I would tell him only to lead and become a CEO if he feels that doing so is the absolutely only way that his deepest desires can become actualized. If he wants such a life, then there is room for him, as there is for lots of young leaders. But the road ahead will be a new path cut with the fresh determination of a generation that dares to find its own way.

MOTION

Think of perspective not as a destination but as a process.

We're not born with perspective. No one can ever get perspective perfectly right. The founders of the world's great wisdom traditions teach us: To know how much we do not know is the beginning of wisdom. There will always be some angle we did not see with absolute clarity. The key here is to hone your intuitive skills daily and have the intention of seeing broadly, and to put that intention into practice through hard work.

The thing about Von Essen's presence is his solidity and good humor in the face of tragedy. We're all human—we all have feet of clay, so we all inevitably crack. Maybe leaders have the perspective to know that it is their job to put themselves and the people following them back together as circumstances demand. Certainly, people would think twice if they thought about the reality of leading, not just the perceived glory of it. Leading is for people who don't turn cracks into occasions for bitterness and self-pity; it's for those people who turn those occasions into moments of transformation.

For the longest time I thought of perspective as an end reward. "When I'm older I'll understand that, or when I'm a father I'll

> *Jon:*
>
> *I think one way to view perspective is to think of it this way: It's like when a clay jug falls off a shelf . . . when glued back together it's going to hold water, but it will remain forever shaped by the memory of its cracks.*

understand that." But change is the constant factor here. There is no way to freeze perspective. We have to adapt and apply knowledge from situation to situation. Perspective is an activity to practice, not a final goal to achieve. Jeff Rich, a young guy, only forty-two, and CEO of ACS, spoke about perspective to the class this way:

> "My perspective—and I think this is a very relevant point when it comes to leadership—is that the future is very uncertain. It has always been uncertain. And it will always be uncertain. The essence of leadership is deciding how to decide what to do in the face of certain uncertainty."

His point made me think of the wise Frances Hesselbein, chairman of the Leader to Leader Institute, who says this about perspective:

> "It is the set of the sails and not the gales that determine the way we go. It may get stormy, [and] there may be some incidents that really shake you up, but you smile, you know what the goal is, and you press on. The gales come and they go, but your eye is fixed on where you are going and nothing deters you . . . if you don't believe this, then every time the wind blows you think

you'll have to stop. Storms come and storms go, but if we know where we're headed there is no problem."

In those moments of storm, the instinct is to stop, to lose resolve, and to put off making decisions until more information is available. But most often, there isn't time for that. And while a quick pause to get your wits about you is always a good idea, you can't stop moving.

AWARENESS

Cultivate the practice of staying alert to your surroundings and to your reactions in those surroundings.

Leaders are put in circumstances that some days are just impossible. In the average workplace, too often people get caught up in the panic of "putting out a fire" without seeking to eradicate its underlying cause. Too frequently we overreact rather than probe—we search for fast answers rather than ask the right questions. Jeff Rich had a great thought that relates directly to this condition:

> "The premise is, the soldiers in the field are always right and the rear generals are always wrong, unless proved otherwise. Give your people in the field the benefit of the doubt for being right. Too often, particularly in large corporations, you end up with a bunch of staffers at corporate second-guessing every decision made out in the field. They're Monday morning quarterbacks."

The goal is to develop a refined and confident gut feel for situations. It doesn't mean being cocky or careless, but it means being certain in that quiet way that admits a clear perspective to wash over you, despite the raging battle outside.

The easiest way to lose perspective is to stay in your office and lose touch with what your clients and customers want and what your employees need. Most senior people admit they're too desk-bound. They don't make a habit of firsthand observing and listening to their value chain and their close-in stakeholders. The only way to feel out the marketplace is to get into it, and to get away from e-mails, voice mails, and trivial meetings.

The same goes for learning how to help your employees perform at their best. I call this "building up your internal radar." When one of your top performers is not contributing as he usually does, you have to take note of it. A leader has to have enough perspective on the work at hand to know when somebody needs a little something extra: a cup of coffee, a few minutes to talk, a lunch out, whatever is required to understand what's going through the mind of a valued employee. Awareness, perspective—they are almost interchangeable. Building up your internal radar is how a leader keeps her people coming to her and trusting her. And people work better for people whom they trust and whom they know care about them.

HONESTY

Tell it like it is. Great leaders are human and do not hide behind their role.

When I asked Fordham leadership speaker Faith Popcorn, the popular culture futurist and adviser to many Fortune 500 companies, who interests her most right now, her answer was blue-collar folks. When I asked her to identify a single leader she truly admires, she said, "I like to watch what the Dalai Lama is doing." Working-class

Americans and a spiritual guide. Old-time values and magnanimous compassion. Those responses were not necessarily what you'd expect to hear even from a futurist.

Faith Popcorn demonstrated in her answers to these questions that her perspective on things was shaped by something beyond, something seemingly unrelated to the consumer trends she predicts. She exemplified that leaders with perspective have the ability to infuse and transcend their personal context right back into their work. What this leader does is integrate observations and her non-business-world perspective into her experience.

During her talk at the Forum, Popcorn spoke about the future trend of what she termed "the transparent corporation," a company that would be accountable to its shareholders in a very open way. Key executives other than just the CEO would be made available to talk to workers and investors at all times. It would be a movement in direct response to the leadership accountability crisis of the last few years—a sort of public truth and reconciliation commission where CEOs would be held accountable on an ongoing basis.

In hearing her talk, something clicked. Was she suggesting that the coming trend, the one that will push business closer to a transparent corporate world, is powered by blue-collar values? And next she made the connection that compassion (as symbolized by the Dalai Lama and his care for the poor and politically oppressed) will impact on the long-term structure of corporate America. Her observation underscores that positive outcomes are interconnected and in relationship with each other and how this makes the world a small place to live in. Because what is more likely than blue-collar values and care for the oppressed coming together, and who better to get it organized than the leaders of the corporate world? Wouldn't that provide a bit of needed perspective?

Von Essen, 9/11, the Dalai Lama, the redefinition of corporate accountability, respect for the American blue-collar worker—

> ## *J o n :*
>
> *When a top consumer futurist is tracking one of the world's foremost yet quietest spiritual leaders, I'm especially intrigued. Can consumer trends have deeper consequences than predicting what people will buy? Are trends indicators of how people are living (or want to live) and the outgrowths of a new orientation to life? Robert Mai and Alan Akerson in their book,* The Leader as Communicator, *say that leaders need to be "linking agents"—listening then relaying what the consumer or customer is telling them.*

they're all related to an emerging new leadership perspective. Faith Popcorn talks about it all the time. It is a perspective that embraces that profit is not the only bottom line, that there are additional bottom lines. Is this an empathetic place to work? Is it a diverse place? Is it a place that does not cause harm to the earth? Is it a place that wants me to bring to work the full weight of my values and humanity? In short, is this a place where I can find leaders who have the courage, the permission, and the authority to humanize the process of work for all people involved?

BALANCE

Steady yourself on both sides of the issue.

When I was coming up, you had mostly men in corporate offices and people of a similar cultural background. No one spoke of personal needs. No one mentioned putting family before work, for fear of being perceived as weak and not fully committed to the company. We buried our feelings and followed our leaders because we wanted to be rewarded and move up. Our leaders did not have to worry about how we personally felt about an issue; such things were irrelevant. The goal was collective forward movement for the business and the company and that was it! About the only kind of perspective we had back then was that if we didn't make the numbers or we lost an opportunity, we just had to keep going, keep moving ahead, no matter what we had to sacrifice to do it.

It's that world, I believe, that kept people like Jonathon out of business. His generation and the one behind his aren't willing to spend their lives that way. They may want to work hard, and they want to learn, but they want a broader context, too—including fulfillment in their personal, not just their professional, lives. The search for this "need fulfillment" brings with it a broader perspective to the notion of the workplace.

In the end, though, leaders can't afford to lose sight of the fact that it's still about business, and that has to be reconciled. We have to make a profit—without that, we disappoint and hurt our stakeholders and employees. One of the seven Becker Values I wrote at the beginning of my tenure at the advertising firm was: We exist to sell our clients' products. I wanted to make clear that we are in the service business, not the self-serving business, and if we ever lose sight of that and keep our focus internal rather than external, the whole thing is gone. In my view, if a client calls at 3 P.M. and wants something at 10 A.M. the next day, I have to have it there—that to me is the perspective called "a client for the long haul."

It was on the issue of balance, on the walk up Bear Mountain, that Jon and I got into our most heated discussion. He argued that while we can't lose sight of profits, this has forever been the only thing corporate America has held dear. That measure alone wasn't enough, he said. His generation saw their parents have no option but to turn their children into latchkey kids. They repeatedly had to make choices between career and family. Jon got adamant that no one should have to make those choices. For him, it had to be both/and, not either/or.

I liked that perspective—his both/and. But isn't our work ethic what makes this country great? Isn't it what has brought about nearly every worthwhile innovation? And let's not forget the shareholders. How are we serving them? Are we bringing them value? Exceeding their expectations and delivering a viable investment for them? We can never let go of thinking about their needs and best interests. We can't sacrifice their investment comfort for our internal personal comfort.

I admit I started to give a bit of a speech here. We both got quiet awhile and continued to walk, following the white blazes up the Appalachian Trail. Jon began again, trying to find a middle ground. He wasn't talking about the office being *Little House on the Prairie,* he said. But he was talking about small shifts that can produce big results—moments when a more rounded perspective is considered. I was able to hear that and let it really sink in. Jon used my own arguments about focus against me and reminded me that there's always a minute . . . thirty seconds at least where a choice is made . . . thirty seconds for some perspective to enter the consideration.

I remember when George Bush, Sr., unwittingly revealed his privileged status to the American people. He had been visiting a grocery store during the 1992 campaign and was bewildered and amazed by the scanner at the checkout counter. This man had been head of the CIA, but he couldn't relate to buying a can of peaches. It's tough to get people to believe you have perspective on how to lead them if you have no idea how they live from day to day.

Jeff Rich said, "The day that your people stop bringing their

POINT/COUNTERPOINT

Sander:

The insistence on work/life balance among young American workers is threatening to catapult American business into a full-blown business leadership crisis. Young people in India and China are not talking about work/life balance or worrying about how to spend more time at home with the kids or to plant a garden. As Thomas L. Friedman points out in his new book The World Is Flat, *people from these countries are economically hungry and extremely competitive. They are developing the kind of work ethic that will soon take them to the next level, where they'll not only be the "outsource" of America-based companies, but the primary "in-source."*

Jon:

My father's concerns regarding work/life balance and its negative impact on competitiveness may not hold up. I think this either/or model sells us short and asks American workers to compromise in ways that are unreasonable.

My father's argument is framed by a particular bottom line—global competitiveness. Jack Welch advocates "making your job so exciting that your personal life becomes a less compelling draw." The idea that negotiating a billion-dollar merger or designing a cutting-edge video game are more compelling draws than reading Goodnight Moon *and snuggling with your child at bedtime is an absurd comparison. These activities are on an entirely different scale. Work without adequate time for intimate connection and personal time has long-term degenerative effects that may not show up on a company profit/loss analysis, but do show up in the character of the people we choose to be and how we model our values for our children.*

problems to you is the day you stop leading. They've either concluded that you don't care about their problems or that you cannot help them." One thing is certain—we don't gain perspective as leaders by living in a vacuum. We have to be in the center of things. We gain perspective by bouncing off the ideas and lives of others.

The issue seems not to be ambition as much as a practical evaluation of what makes the best formula for balance of work and home. To define a good leader nowadays, there are fewer stereotypes, fewer "musts." It's not solely about schooling, background, age, and connections. It is about becoming unilateral and performance-based. Leadership is forward moving—if your perspective is stuck back somewhere ten years ago, your people have probably stopped listening to you and your company is on its way to has-been status. Awareness, awareness, awareness.

Jonathon's Perspective

> When it is dark enough, you can see the stars.
> —CHARLES A. BEARD

I grew up not far from Bear Mountain. I used to go there as a child all the time with my family. In winter, we'd go to ice skate or, if there was enough snow, to sled. We drank hot chocolate in the lodge and looked at the motorized holiday decorations inside glass cases. Growing up, my family didn't hike or camp, so a place like Bear Mountain was really just a winter place for us.

When I became a teenager, though, Bear Mountain became a place I'd go during all seasons, just so I could hike. The Appalachian Trail runs right through it, and that's amazing to me—a 2,100-mile foot trail from Georgia to Maine running right through my backyard. My friend Tom and I used to talk about walking the whole trail, though we haven't . . . yet. Bear Mountain was the place where I started to think about hitting the open road—seeing just how big the world was outside my little corner of it. It was where I camped for the first time and noticed how truly miraculous the stars were at night. It was the place where my perspective began to open . . . and once that occurs there is no going back.

In the woods, Dad spoke to me about Tom Von Essen with great admiration. Focusing on Von Essen's story helps to ground my perspective of leadership—first of all because a city employee does not make a lot of money, and second, because Von Essen was never motivated by luxury. He was motivated by camaraderie and a willingness to serve something greater than himself. Leading isn't for everyone; just watch American television commercials for five minutes and you'll see that luxury is the perceived good that people want. They want things to come easy.

But leadership doesn't come easy. It is a hard practice. And my father makes the point that any material reward that comes from it needs to be seen for what it is—a side effect, not a motivating cause. To me, this distinction is crucial. You have to enjoy the work itself because the activity of leading ranks above the reward. Von Essen loved being a firefighter and he wanted to make firefighting better for the people he worked with—that's why he became a leader.

When I interviewed Bruce Tulgan, one of the country's leading generational experts and best-selling author of *Winning the Talent Wars,* on the subject of balance, he told me:

> "Xers think work [and] life balance obviously. They will shop for a job [or a] manager where they have more control of where, when, how they work. They will give up money and other rewards for more control over where/when/how."

I find this desire for balance to be true for my own situation and many of my friends. My sister, Pamela Weinberg, is a prime

example. Before having her children, she was a full-time PR executive on the fast track. She had planned on going back to work after
having kids, but something incredibly fortuitous happened instead.
As she was trying to navigate the delights and perils of raising a
baby in New York City, she began to scoop up every piece of information available. In fairly short order, she realized there was no
single source to inform her of the best place to buy a crib, meet
other new moms, find a baby-friendly restaurant, and on and on.
Despair? Not Pamela. She went out and created it. She researched
and cowrote *City Baby,* a compendium of all the resources and
accompanying insights of raising a baby in the Big Apple. The book
is now in its fourth edition, with Chicago, Boston, and LA editions
as well.

Pamela turned herself into new mom consultant—writing articles, giving weekly seminars, doing TV talk shows, but on a part-
time basis. Because Pamela knew that she could not "have it all"—a
full-time career and being a wife and mother—she opened herself
to finding an entirely new career that has blossomed into a life
mission of helping new moms everywhere navigate the amazing and
rocky road of child rearing.

The trick, as my father indicated, is figuring out how to both
"do life" and "do business" well. For Dad's generation and the
boomer generation, there was a flagrant conflict. When I asked
Bruce Tulgan to enlighten me on this, he told me about a comment
he received from a summer intern when he recently addressed a
large accounting and consulting firm. The intern said: "What I
want is to do work that is really interesting and meaningful, and I
don't mind working hard, but I want to do it on my own time. I
want to work, when I'm feeling inspired. . . . And I also need to
work with really smart people that I like a lot . . . in a great company in a location that's a fun place to live . . . where I'm learning
every day. . . ." At first he started to laugh. He thought the kid was

joking. But then Tulgan looked around the room and noticed that he was the only one laughing.

Young people today work incredibly hard, gather top credentials, do very well in the interview process, and demonstrate that they can ably perform. In the old days, Tulgan said, this was the group that would work like dogs around the clock. Do the grunt work. Be miserable. Travel until they unravel. Do what they're told. Sacrifice everything about their personal lives for as long as it takes to reap the rewards of the internal hierarchy of the organization. But that is not the business-as-usual case anymore. Those days are fading fast.

These young people and many of their peers throughout the world are reinventing success. They don't plan to go after it the old-fashioned way because paying your dues, climbing the ladder, and wrapping your whole life around a one-size-fits-all career path is anathema to them. No way are they signing up to be workaholics, and they have the market muscle to resist and chart their own course. "Are these young folks going to grow up and get realistic?" Tulgan rhetorically asked. "Don't kid yourself."

To lead this creative class of workers, Tulgan believes in a methodology that he has termed HOT Management, an acronym for hands-on and transactional. "The fundamental principle of HOT Management is that supervisory management nowadays is to be 'transactional,' rather than hierarchical," says Tulgan. "That means there is a quid pro quo for everything: If employees want rewards, they must perform. The more employees perform the more rewards they receive. And high performance is the only measure. Equally important is the emphasis on being hands-on, rather than hands-off [management]. If managers are going to be transactional, they must be extremely knowledgeable about the work their direct reports are doing They must spend a lot of time spelling out expectations, clarifying standards, and defining goals and deadlines. And they must have the guts to hold employees accountable."

What a different world from the one my father came up in. The power resides with the indispensable worker, not the employer. And, as Tulgan explains it, the employer can no longer expect workers to fit into an established corporate hierarchy; rather, employers should be prepared to customize the work environment to suit the needs of their people. I obviously like this shift because it puts people first, bureaucracy second. I have no illusions, however, that this shift in perspective is occurring because corporate America has become "kinder and gentler." I know it is occurring simply because the economics have shifted. Yet, regardless of cause, economics do eventually affect attitude.

In today's economy, there is no such thing as long-term job security, so we might as well tie rewards to consistent short-term performance. In a way, this situation looks incredibly rosy for the young professional because she can design her own job description and hours. But in another way it is incredibly tenuous, because there is no guarantee of long-term job security.

Helen Keller said, "It is pathetic when a person has sight, but no vision." And in the end, that is what perspective means to me—to have empathy, to see others as being as human as you are. My dad and I, through writing this book, have been able to do this in a very personal way. I can really feel for all the long hours he had to put in over the course of his career and how painful it was for him to miss so much outside work in the process. And he can see how difficult it is for me to work without any real hope of job security—to go from one performance to another without a guarantee. And the more we understand, the more we can tune in to each other and move past our differences and toward a shared higher purpose. Perspective is the ability to take it all in and not rush to judgment. It is a practice that takes lots of practice. You never finally arrive there . . . the rug is always being pulled out from under you. So I agree with Dad here when he says that the practice of perspective is about "awareness, awareness, awareness. . . ."

Here's a closing thought. I wrote this chapter while listening to Louis Armstrong and Ella Fitzgerald sing a particularly funny version of a classic tune about two people who see the world differently. I laughed when Armstrong said tomato and Fitzgerald said tomahto. It's amazing the stink we can make about things like how we pronounce a word. But we do that—we get stuck in thinking we're right and they're wrong. My suggestion when that happens: Laugh heartily at your own foolishness. Without laughter, doing this book wouldn't have been nearly as fun. Not only that, it wouldn't have broadened our perspective nearly as much. One of the things that separates us human beings from the other species is our ability to laugh—there is something almost divine in it. It returns us to a kind of innocence. A good belly laugh bathes us in new perspective. For Dad and me, it definitely was the laughter at how we pronounced our differences that got us through the temptation to "call the whole thing off." So at work, remember to joke around. It's good for your perspective and your prospects.

PERSPECTIVE

Checklist for Leaders

Practice/Activity

❑ Activity
The ultimate reward of leadership is the activity itself.

❑ Motion
Think of perspective not as a destination but as a process.

❑ Awareness
Cultivate the practice of staying alert to your surroundings and to your reactions in those surroundings.

❑ Honesty
Tell it like it is. Great leaders are human and do not hide behind their role.

❑ Balance
Steady yourself on both sides of the issue.

CHAPTER 7

PARANOIA

Never Take Your Eye off the Ball

We have to behave as though ten fiery demons are chasing us at
all times . . . our biggest enemies are arrogance and complacency.
—JEFF BLEUSTEIN, CEO HARLEY-DAVIDSON

Success at leadership brings a sense of accomplishment. Failure at leadership
can be detrimental to the leader, harmful to followers, and disastrous to
organizations.—DONALD E. MCHUGH, *Golf and the Game of Leadership*

Jon and I spent the last few days of our walk on the golf courses of
Eastern Long Island. Jon has played golf off and on ever since he
was eight. He always had a feel for the game . . . though he has
never taken it very seriously. Jon just likes to be out there. He says
that what he still likes about golf is that its structure forces you to
focus on only one thing at time. You cannot take two shots at once.
Jon tries not to play against anyone when he plays golf, not even
himself.

The story with me and golf is very different. Golf has been an
agonizing nonskill of mine since I've been about forty. I take lessons, watch videos, subscribe to *Golf Digest,* buy newfangled clubs,
and own an array of golf shirts from every course I've played. Has
all this activity made a bit of difference? Not much. A couple of
years ago when Jon and I were in South Carolina for a family vaca-
tion, he, my wife Mechele, and I went out to play golf. I hated my
swing all day. Even after eighteen holes in the heat, I went to the

driving range to hit a bucket of balls so I could "fix" my swing. Jon and Mechele went back to the house to tell everybody I might be a little late to my birthday dinner. Nobody said a word—they know me all too well!

I'll probably never be a great golfer. But what I have excelled at is recruiting great people who have helped me build a great company. I'm good at this for exactly the same reasons that I'm a mediocre golfer—I think about it all the time. I never stop thinking about all the aspects of my business and how to improve its performance, about all the things that might go wrong even when all signs are clear skies. I focus on the mechanics of how things are working. I do not let things "take care of themselves." I know that if you let things take care of themselves they will simply disappear into the ether. Or worse, your clients, employees, and your value chain will find somewhere else to go, somewhere where someone is staying focused on their needs.

I view my job as making sure things are being taken care of.

Jon:

When we're on the course, I encourage Dad to just let his swing "be"—to not think about it so much. But he can't help thinking about all the elements that constitute his swing and how to configure those elements into a straight ball that flies long to the middle of the fairway. Dad's rational vigilance to every detail doesn't work on the golf course as well as swinging into the flow of the moment might. I, on the other hand, get in the "flow" and frequently miss plenty of details along the way. We could stand to rub off on each other a bit.

Am I paranoid about making my business and myself the absolute best? Do I obsess and try to do everything in my power to ensure positive outcomes for my clients and their customers, for my employees and for myself? Absolutely! Does this same kind of paranoia I bring to business help me on the golf course? Don't I wish it did! But after forty years in business, it's the only way I know how to be.

Jonathon and others of his generation don't see the same necessity for paranoia (or hypervigilance) as I do. They see this way of working as an interruption of the balance they are trying to cultivate between life and work. Jon and I have agreed to disagree on this point, understanding and learning from each other's views as we work our way through the golf courses on the South Fork of Long Island.

From my vantage point, I think you should be attuned to the knowledge that, at any time, every competitor of yours is out to recruit your best people, steal your ideas, take over your customers, and reinvent and improve your products. I recommend allowing for the worst-case scenario to propel you to be better today than you were yesterday. Whether you're in the world of business, academia, organized labor, or nonprofits, a touch of paranoia is a valuable trait. The word tends to give us a jolt, and it's meant to do that. To maintain a healthy competitive edge, a leader takes into account the possibility of her organization being spied on, stolen from, plagiarized, and copied. We call it paranoia; you can call it hypervigilance or "high alert" status—it doesn't matter, as long as you embed it into your organization's culture as an antidote to complacency.

LISTEN AND ACT

Solicit feedback personally from big and small customers and employees. Develop your business intelligence network. Do not rely on "reports."

With total candor we heard from Raul Cesan about how he temporarily took his eye off the ball of GMP (good manufacturing practices) when he was at Schering-Plough, and how it cost him. He said to the Fordham Leadership Forum:

> "I completely missed it! I should have brought in outside consultants once a year to tell me whether the industry's GMP standards had been raised. I did that in every other area. I had external auditors and consultants—had them in IT, and we were truly ahead of the curve there. I'd bring in McKinsey [consultants] every six months and I brought in IBM, too. I had all my operations raked over and examined. All of them, that is, except manufacturing. There I made a cardinal error. I did not follow Ronald Reagan's rule when dealing with the Russians: TRUST, BUT VERIFY."

Cesan explained how over a ten-year period there was never the slightest hint that there was a manufacturing problem at Schering. Until two years before the manufacturing problem surfaced, Food and Drug Administration (FDA) inspectors were actually being trained in Schering's facilities. That fact provided Cesan with a false sense of security. He had formed a crack team that developed the corporation's state-of-the art manufacturing facility, and that team never changed. This did not turn out to be a good thing. The team did not go outside to update its practices and did not bring in enough outsiders to check on the facility. And so Raul Cesan learned (was admittedly shocked to learn) that his company's one-time state-of-the-art manufacturing facility now needed major up-grades.

Cesan wasn't paranoid about manufacturing at his company, just everything else. He thought he had manufacturing locked up. The lesson: You never have anything finally all locked up. All things are constantly in flux and need to be updated, examined, and tested on a continual basis. Raul Cesan is such a great leadership model for us because he is willing to admit his errors and not disguise them. He teaches from his successes as well as from his mistakes. Most of the time, our mistakes teach us a lot more than our suc-cesses.

RAISE THE BAR

Don't wait for your customers, clients, employees, or the rest of your value chain to demand more of you. Expect more of yourself and deliver it. Keep the edge.

If I had to put a warning label on this leadership P it would read "May cause some sleepless nights," but that's the price sometimes. It never matters to me how long a team works on a new concept for a client. If it isn't absolutely through-the-roof, knock-your-socks-off great, I don't want the client to see it. I value my reputa-tion and never want people to say: "That Flaum, his work is usually good." A reputation like that puts you in the pile with everyone else, and you can't lead when you're just like everybody else. You have to over-deliver every time. The client needs to be excited and resold again and again and again—at every new product launch, with every new campaign, and with every new product concept.

Jeff Rich, the CEO of Affiliated Computer Services (ACS), has the attitude that yesterday's success is tomorrow's expected standard. He continually plans and strategizes to raise the bar on whatever business process outsourcing service ACS is delivering. ACS does back-office business services more efficiently than its clients can achieve internally. Rich's employees can do it better because they think about it relentlessly. He says: "Be it a human resources function, an accounting function, or a New York E-ZPass function—[for example] how to collect money, how to improve the collection rates, how to get the bills out faster, how to get the money moving faster—we lay awake at night thinking about that kind of thing."

Being complacently "good" usually means that you're on the way out. Being excellent in a new surprising way means you're on the move. If you find yourself standing still you're probably slipping. Do you have to be relentless about examining the quality of your own work and the people who work for you? Yes. Coasting is just not an option. In the end, people will thank you for this kind of vigilance. It may create great angst, but along with it emerges better war stories of battles won.

DEVELOP A POSITIVE RELATIONSHIP WITH FEAR

Identify what keeps you up at night and proactively do something about it.

If you think paranoia makes sense for advertising and business process outsourcing, you better believe it is crucial for science and technology. Gregory Young, the CEO of CorePharma, told the Fordham Leadership Forum about a former Baxter Laboratories colleague he worked with for nine years. This associate ran the medication delivery business.

This man suffered from a recurring fear. He envisioned that instead of using bags to deliver sterile water intravenously (of which Baxter sells over one million annually), hospitals would install a little tap by the patient's bed from which sterile water would flow, just like oxygen does. So every year he called together all the key people at Baxter for a meeting, including top experts, to report on who was closest to producing sterile water from a tap. To avoid that day—the day Baxter will be reduced to being the owner of a $500 million "garage" in North Carolina for warehousing intravenous bags, rather than a state-of-the-art health product manufacturer—that guy at Baxter stayed on the lookout to protect the assets of his business.

There are plenty of companies that tell themselves that their technology will have a good run for the next five to ten years, that they're ahead of the curve of change. Then, bang, they get walloped.

Dell Inc. is the antithesis to this condition. Michael Dell fights complacency at every turn. He runs one of the few companies that have made custom selling on the Internet a high-profit business. Every day, the company delivers on the promise that consumers can personally design the exact computer they need, then Dell will build it for them. Dell is so far ahead of the competition because Michael Dell revolutionized his industry doing precisely what Fordham leader Jeff Rich says must be done—meeting client expectations, raising the bar on service delivered to them, and then maintaining your advantage again and again and again and again—constantly reinventing the standards before the customer grows bored with Dell service.

Paranoia has nothing to do with hierarchy or position and everything to do with hard work and innovation—creating things that don't already exist and taking existing things and making them better. Senator John Glenn told us that some leaders are simply leaders because they are so far ahead of everybody else. They become experts in areas where others don't have a clue. He mentioned Albert Einstein as an example. So what if the great scientist couldn't match his socks or make change; the man understood the universe in a way that nobody else could get their head around.

Jim Roberts is steps ahead of the competition because of his vigilant study and observation. Jon introduced me to Roberts's work, and I found his story instructive about how young leaders are applying hypervigilance in the open field of regional economic development. The twenty-nine-year-old Roberts founded a company called First Round out of Charlotte, North Carolina. The mission of the company was to link selected entrepreneurs with innovative ideas to the venture capitalists that would help them grow their ideas into globally competitive companies. Roberts doesn't miss an article or a study in print, online, or in the far reaches of academia if it is concerned with the theme of regional economic development. He understands the speed at which things change, and he knows that in business, being right isn't enough, but what often makes the difference is being right first. Many new companies were built in Charlotte because of Roberts's ability not just to size up the direction of the economy, but also to react swiftly and creatively in a field that shifts without warning. While his company was creating dynamic start-ups, the state of North Carolina was losing tens of thousands of manufacturing jobs first to Mexico and then to India and China. Known for his remarkable success in business development in the private sector, Roberts next found himself enmeshed in the specific challenges Western North Carolina was facing. After a couple of years, he closed First Round and moved to Asheville as executive director of the nonprofit Blue Ridge Entrepreneurial Council (BREC) and the Blue Ridge Angel Investors Network (BRAIN).

Now thirty-four, Roberts educates first-time entrepreneurs

about the realities of finding investors, while he creates mentoring and networking opportunities, provides biweekly written communications that keep entrepreneurs energized and up-to-date with regional and national news that affects them, and helps qualified entrepreneurs through the capital formation and preparation process. Jim Roberts is helping North Carolina to grow an eclectic economy by using his own brand of paranoia to ensure that the region makes the most of its prized assets: its creative people and its sought-after quality of life. This is not an easy task in a region so hard hit with manufacturing job losses and one that has no private venture capital funds. But these challenges seem to spur Roberts on to greater success. His mission is to transform raw talent into economic infrastructure, and he has made a great start of it in a short time. One of the secrets to his success is never letting up and being paranoid about protecting the assets he has been entrusted with.

PAY ATTENTION TO ANOMALIES

If it seems "weird," it just might be important. Investigate!

If we can name the enemies of this leadership P as arrogance and complacency, then we can call its friends open-mindedness and forward movement. And this brings me back to culture watcher and trend spotter Faith Popcorn, because she is constantly asking Fortune 500 companies to open their eyes and see what they would prefer to dismiss.

Big companies bring in Popcorn and her team at BrainReserve to look for the demons that might take their company down. Popcorn has been talking to food companies about children's health for a long time. Obesity is one of the top-ten leading causes of death in this country. Childhood obesity is out of control. It's been making headlines for years now, but even back when it wasn't, Faith Popcorn was talking to consumers and health professionals and reading the studies in health and medical journals and telling food companies about them. She was telling them that the days of high-sugar diets were soon coming to an end and that they'd better prepare for it. A few companies listened some years ago, and their products are solid today, while other companies are running to catch up because the paranoia bogeyman did in fact exist.

I find the work she does so compelling because she waves a flag that signals, "Look over here and see what is actually happening in our culture. Get out of your office and go to a supermarket, a school, a health clinic, a car dealership, anywhere your consumer is spending her time; see it for yourself, up close and real!" She knows that if her clients don't do it today, that their competitors will outflank them tomorrow.

When Popcorn was a girl, she used to sit with her grandfather outside his haberdashery store. They would sit on the curb and look at the display window. When customers passed the window and didn't stop, her grandfather knew that the ties had to be repositioned, and he taught that lesson to his granddaughter. Together they would change the ties, how they were positioned on the shirts, maybe even change the colors of the shirts, and then continue to watch how potential customers reacted. "I learned an important marketing lesson very early," Popcorn told the Forum students. "That it's not what you've got, but how you're positioned that counts. And of course, a big part of positioning is seeing the future. How can you know how a product should be, if you don't have some thoughts about what is going to happen tomorrow?" Faith Popcorn makes sure that her clients are paranoid about the future. She takes them out on the proverbial curb and sits with them and watches with them as customers or potential customers do or don't pass by their store window.

There is an inherent openness to Popcorn's methodology. She doesn't force-fit trends—they are what they are. Her contribution is that she is unafraid to notice it, investigate it, and provide new insights about it. She told us:

> "Most people, they see something weird and they just wipe it away [by saying] 'That's weird.' It doesn't fit, so they don't have to pay attention to it. But this is the wrong approach. When you see something 'weird,' record it, examine it, turn it over in your mind a thousand times, because it's pointing to something— something on the brink of happening that can change the way you live and the way you do business."

Faith Popcorn shows companies that they aren't being nearly paranoid enough, particularly about their women consumer constituencies. She constantly has to challenge corporate America to pay more than lip service to this powerful group of decision makers. Corporations say they do, but they don't, and then they are surprised when female consumers use their friends, detractor websites or blogs, and other more personal sources, to check out brand reliability. In today's world, often the last one to be trusted is the manufacturer. If you're a competent, reliable producer of goods, that can make you feel spied on and just a little paranoid. But attention must be paid to the ever-growing number of critics.

Faith Popcorn is someone who gets our paranoia revved up. She cites the research and predicts the trends that have shown the size and scope of this huge and changing global marketplace where everyone with a dollar has a voice. People vote with their dollars and those kind of elections happen daily, with some companies left standing and others (often the ones that don't worry about competition) lurking in the shadows, fading out of sight.

WATCH YOUR BACK

*Watch things big and small because until
the mistake happens, you never really know
which was "big" and which was "small."*

This leadership P has everything to do with seeing and doing what matters, so I turn again to Randy Thurman, the former top gun pilot and current CEO and chairman of VIASYS Healthcare. Thurman makes a direct connection between combat and leadership:

> "The best fighter pilots that I knew were able to weed through a tremendous amount of input and information—air speed, angle of attack, where the enemy is, where the ground fire is coming from, how the engines are performing, how much fuel you have left before you're going to run out, a thousand things at 600 miles an hour—[and] make decisions and act upon them. And in my observation, that's what the best leaders can do."

Top gun pilots have to be cognizant of absolutely everything and need to be faster, more observant, more calculating, more aware, and more paranoid than their adversary. You could almost say that these pilots see and hear things that no one else does. The skills Thurman learned as a fighter pilot are what he refers to as "making it through the OODA loop." The U.S. Air Force commissioned a study of why certain pilots make it to the level of fighter pilots and others do not. The finding was that it came down to the OODA loop and how fast a pilot could get through it. The acronym refers to the ability to 1) observe, 2) orient, 3) decide, and 4) act. In the first phase, the pilot must quickly size up a situation. In the second, he must get in full control of that situation to the best of his ability, preempting a move by the enemy if necessary. In the third phase, the pilot must be able to make faster and better decisions than his opponent. By the fourth phase, he has to be ready to act without hesitation. The reality is that the cycle happens while flying at 600 miles per hour, in the blink of an eye, similar to the speed at which a client walks out the door or how long it takes your company to be trumped by a superior product.

Why compare the heightened awareness of a combat fighter pilot to the positive paranoia of a business, government, or non-profit leader? Is in fact the fighter pilot being paranoid? After all, he has a real enemy aiming to shoot him down before he gets shot. That's exactly the point. The leader isn't really being particularly paranoid, either; the leader is simply being realistic about the effort required to win.

What we term *paranoia* is also in many leaders' view a name for competitive advantage. Thurman commented to my students that whereas business decision making was once thought of as a chess game, the more apt analogy today is one of a dogfight. He described a global market that I know all too well. He talked about a market where product cycles are short and the winner of the latest product war takes all. "You have to look at your competitor as an enemy and expect to kill or be killed," he said. "You stay alive in a market like this one dogfight at a time." The advice to "watch your back" is an understatement.

What Thurman calls the OODA leader and I call the paranoid leader gets you to the same place: A leader observes what the competition is doing and organizes development strategies to stay one step ahead. A leader knows his customers' needs and constantly works to exceed expectations, not just consistently meet them. A leader strives to hire people that he trusts so decision-making authority is granted at the lowest levels of the organization. Such authority allows employees to nip a competitive problem in the bud, encouraging leadership as way of life in the organization.

What emerges from this analysis is that to be a leader, you have to always be one step ahead of the competition. And to do that in today's world, you must be immersed in the best information available. There is no margin for error in this dogfight. If you take your eye off the situation for a second, it can move completely out of your hands and you are simply playing a game of reactive catch-up. And that can make you paranoid.

Jonathon's Perspective

Let us not look back in anger or forward in fear, but around in awareness.
—James Thurber

We don't see things as they are; we see them as we are.
—Anaïs Nin

Paranoia is the leadership P that makes me the most uncomfortable. Human beings can become paranoid pretty easily. It is a quality we do not have to work too hard at to cultivate. The world of business sometimes lends itself to the language of a war—"competitive advantage," "our company's arsenal," "the war room," "hostile takeover"—and that's tough for me to get on board with.

My generation has a different way of working. It is based on awareness, not paranoia. For me, paranoia has negative side effects, and if I can avoid them I'd like to. The older generation that mastered this quality suffers the consequences of its side effects: a constant low-grade tension and reactivity that has become synonymous with work ethic and commitment.

My dad is onto something very important in his acknowledgment of our need to develop a positive relationship with fear. I just want to propose a slightly adjusted commentary to how we approach fear at work. Rather than always practice control, I advocate using acceptance from time to time. In many of the cases cited here, the relationship with fear is to project those fears onto future events and be vigilantly prepared to combat them if and when they arise—to see the future as riddled with potential problems. We seem to leave out the notion that our actions and study can better prepare us to deal with reality's curveballs. We invest in believing that our paranoia can prevent unpredictable things from showing up, but often this is an illusion. Paranoia works . . . sometimes. But it robs us of fully enjoying those times when everything is just fine. When a problem shows up that we were paranoid about, we have two problems to deal with: our tension that our paranoia sustains and the actual problem itself.

Paranoia implies placing a certain lens on reality—one that sees clouds even on a day of clear skies. I don't propose putting on rose-colored glasses. I see simple awareness, doing our best to be fully cognizant of our environment, as the antidote. This can be done with calm attention. We can see a problem at work as something not to attack but to transform. In reality, both paranoia and calm awareness probably work equally as well in preempting a potential disaster. Who would disagree that the side effects of the latter are so much more preferable?

My Tai Chi teacher, Shifu Derek Croley, who spent a good bit of time studying in China, asks our class to stay focused on cultivating our "creative mind," not our "competitive mind." Founded in China as a physical manifestation of Taoist philosophy, the focus of the Tai Chi art is on balance and energy (*chi*). The slow choreographed, swanlike movements improve balance and serve as a moving meditation. The art was created traditionally as a way to do combat if an enemy attacked. The notion is to use the person's hostile (i.e., out of balance) energy against them. So if you are attacked there is no true counterattack, there is only the redirection of energy such that the aggressor has his own aggression turned on himself.

The part of Tai Chi in which we practice with another's energy is called the "pushing hands" exercise. We close our eyes and stand face-to-face with our partner with hands lightly touching. The idea is to experience the energy of the other person and respond. If they push hard you push soft and redirect without resistance. If your partner is pushing softly and trying to draw you off balance, you are firmer. It goes on this way, with eyes closed, as you begin to feel the subtle energy of your partner's movements. It is said that after years of practice you can feel what your partner is going to do before he ever makes the move. (I haven't advanced to this level yet.) I have found that being in tune with another person's sense of balance, as well as my own, produces a quiet awareness akin to meditation. It is in this space that my teacher encourages "creative mind." We are urged to forget about knocking our partner off balance or somehow "winning" and are instead encouraged to cultivate enough awareness to move beyond any notion of competition and simply arrive at a new kind of creative interaction.

When I transfer this teaching about pushing hands to paranoia in business, I'm immediately struck by the importance of intimacy. Without close, almost intuitive contact, you would be lost in this exercise. What does this mean for dealing with competitors in business? It means doing all you can to know them extremely well. It means respecting their ability to throw you off balance at any time with a surprise move. It means you can never forget about them or take their movements for granted. It means you can never underestimate them.

My father and I agree on this point, but how to function with it is where we differ. Like in pushing hands, the key is intimacy. It is about developing an attitude of not fearing the opponent and reacting, but instead feeling the opponent and transcending. This takes practice, awareness, and confidence. Will most of us react first and fall into "competitive mind"? Absolutely. We were culturally conditioned to behave that way. But over time, Tai Chi says we can catch ourselves and move into another way of relating to competition that allows for the grip of paranoia to loosen.

My father's brand of paranoia sees this state of affairs as a competition. His tradition is firmly rooted in the competitive mind-set: Focus on staying or becoming number one. But we could just as easily view this as a sort of dance that is the very nature of capitalist business—an ongoing meditation that is simply part of our business life. How do we live with this state of affairs creatively, rather than combatively, is my question.

PARANOIA

Checklist for Leaders

Practice/Activity

❏ Listen and Act
Solicit feedback personally from big and small customers and employees. Develop your business intelligence network. Do not rely on "reports."

❏ Raise the Bar
Don't wait for your customers, clients, employees, and the rest of the value chain to demand more of you. Expect more of yourself and deliver it. Keep the edge.

❏ Develop a Positive Relationship with Fear
Identify what keeps you up at night and proactively do something about it.

❏ Pay Attention to Anomalies
If it seems "weird," it just might be important. Investigate!

❏ Watch Your Back
Watch things big and small because until the mistake happens, you never really know which was "big" and which was "small."

CHAPTER 8

PRINCIPLES

A Leader's Cornerstone

There are times when you devote yourself to a higher
cause than personal safety.—SENATOR JOHN GLENN

Our values are woven from the innermost strands of our lives.
—FRANCES HESSELBEIN, CHAIRMAN OF THE BOARD, LEADER TO LEADER INSTITUTE

I can see Jon's point about quiet places. The open air gives you a chance to reflect and breathe deeper. In the city, I don't notice the birds much. Out here on this Blue Ridge Mountain trail, I hear their calls and my own footsteps and hear Jon's out in front. It's been raining on and off and that makes the rocks slippery. Jon goes first and waits for me. He sticks out his hand now and then, in case I need it to balance myself on the climb. It is a peculiar thing to grab the hand of your son for balance when you're the one who taught him to walk.

When we get to the top, Jon says I'll see how the whole walk was worth it, rain and all. I have always known that getting through something rough has its rewards. And most of the time it's not the goal but the doing itself that's the real reward. I think that may be because it allows us to exercise and test out our integrity and credibility. And once we've established that we trust ourselves, it's not far from the realization that we are someone to be trusted and can, in fact, lead others.

It's easier to define what principles are not, than what they are. To understand the notion of principles, you have to practice the behaviors that demonstrate integrity and credibility in all matters and actions. Principles attain traction when they get exercised often. Think of *principles* not just as noun but as a verb—an action word. Principles don't serve well as relics that you dust off once a year at an annual meeting and then shelve when you come back to the "real work" at hand. Principles are the real work of leadership. Without actively engaging principles in everyday situations, leaders have no legs to stand on. Eventually, they go down.

One event that particularly lit up the Fordham Leadership Forum was the talk by Christine Poon, worldwide chairperson of medicines and nutritionals Johnson & Johnson. Poon spoke with no notes. Her focus was on values. In her earlier career she had worked at Squibb, a pharmaceutical powerhouse of the 1980s with a value system that stated that "the priceless ingredient of every company is the honor and integrity of its maker." Poon's experience was that "a company's values can provide a powerful inspiration and ultimately shape everything about the company."

In her post at J&J, she is one of the highest-ranking women and a major player among the big names in the pharmaceutical industry. Poon told us one of the reasons she was drawn to J&J is that the company truly walks its talk. Decisions big and little revolve around its credo, even in today's challenging and challenged marketplace.

What resonated for her is that J&J's credo starts with customers—namely, patients—not, she emphasized, with value for the shareholders. At J&J, the belief is that if patients are well served, the shareholders will be, too. Written by General Robert Johnson, the company's founder, the credo states J&J's responsibility as follows:

> The number-one responsibility is first to the customer (doctors, nurses, patients), then to employees, the community you work in, and finally to shareholders.

Poon's advice to the class: Whether you are in an entrepreneurial job or corporate, think about your values. Think about the values you want to live by and then find a place to work that shares your values.

A leader can't lead without followers. And you can't have followers without having integrity and credibility. You can be called president, publisher, chancellor, principal, director, prime minister . . . it doesn't matter; if you don't have integrity and credibility, people may go through the motions to your face but behind your back, they'll undermine you, scoff at your declarations, and never really align with you. Well, maybe they'll appear to be in your corner when it is expedient, such as for some short-term, self-interest goal that they have, but when it comes to real loyalty and getting behind you and fighting for your cause in a crunch . . . forget it.

When Jeff Rich, CEO of ACS, visited the Fordham Leadership Forum, he put up a slide of a recent *New Yorker* cartoon. The caption read: "A recent poll shows more people believe in Santa Claus than CEOs." The class broke up with laughter, even more so because I had just gotten through introducing Rich as a veteran CEO of a publicly traded company (which raised a few young eyebrows). Like Rich, you've got to be able to laugh at yourself—especially if you're the leader. He is a good role model for that because he possesses a healthy dose of self-esteem. Rich told our class that during the heart of the CEO scandals (his company is based in Texas, just like Enron), he started introducing himself at cocktail parties as "one of those scumbag public company CEOs." He said it always got a laugh, or at the very least the comment interrupted the rush to judgment from first impressions that a lot of us too often make.

CREDIBILITY

Be honest with and thoughtful of your people.
Admit mistakes readily.

There was a time when a CEO of a publicly traded company was thought of with the highest regard. The CEO was someone accountable to shareholders and charged with upholding the public trust. The chief executive was a person accountable for millions or even billions of dollars in revenue and earnings; a person responsible for employing a workforce as large as a small town, sometimes larger; a person who ought to be someone you can count on for being honest, thoughtful, and community-minded. In the recent past, this concept has been turned on its head. Instead, some CEOs have taken to indulging their personal predilections, to packing their board of directors with cronies who rubberstamp bad decisions or who look the other way when actions are taken that hurt long-term profitability.

The concept of the board of directors was supposed to be that it functioned as overseer, to hold in check a CEO's ego, to help the organization rank high among its peers, to represent the voice of the smallest shareholder. However, the corporate boardroom has failed us in large measure as an objective form of governance. When the compensation committee cuts the CEO an absurd exit package time and again, we know we are courting danger. The heads of Fannie Mae, Enron, Healthsouth, WorldCom, the New York Stock Exchange (NYSE), Tyco, and all the others thought leadership gave them special privileges. They thought it gave them the opportunity to cash in for their personal benefit. They didn't practice the values inherent in leadership—although they spoke it constantly in their talks to shareholders and others. Even if heads of companies aren't outright juggling numbers, if they are asking for and receiving big compensation packages while their people aren't getting raises or bonuses, they've missed the boat.

A public company means a public trust, and shareholders are corporate citizens who are supposed to benefit from the decisions and actions of their company leaders. If those leaders and members of their staffs prove themselves to be ethically inept, "stockholder citizens" lose faith. Lost faith fuels nonviolent revolution—stock once valued and depended upon gets devalued and often sold. If, indeed, greed becomes the basis for attaining a leadership position, it worries me that this perception will become overblown and will result in people no longer valuing or even believing in their investment in corporate America.

If that scenario plays out, the days of this country's leadership in industry and innovation may be numbered. What worries me further is that even with the enactment of Sarbanes-Oxley, young people will connect salaried work, particularly big corporate endeavors, with inevitably becoming unprincipled. How will organizations, corporations, and nonprofits demonstrate that there are still many more companies that practice integrity and credibility daily than ones that don't? They just don't make the news. The corporate leadership crisis has made it so much more imperative to stress awareness of the people who do their jobs day in and day out while abiding by principles, and to learn their practices and coping mechanisms.

One such CEO who has operated under the umbrella of credibility over the course of his career is Bill George, former CEO of

Medtronic and the author of the 2003 book, *Authentic Leadership.* George has been a strong voice for stricter and more neutral corporate governance, even while serving on the boards of three of the world's most powerful companies—Goldman Sachs, Target Corporation, and Novartis. If you are a CEO, George stresses the importance of listening to your conscience, rather than worrying about the security analysts. In the September 2004 issue of *Fast Company,* George commented: "It's in your ear all the time, them [the security analysts] saying, 'This is what you have to do to boost the stock.' Leaders start responding to that instead of listening to their own voice." It was Bill George who coined the expression *short termitis* as a moniker for CEOs and boards that are so fearful of disappointing the analysts that they do something that's not in the long-term best interest of their company. Principles are not short-term action!

George is a leader who is not at all interested in expediency. He has gone out on limb after limb and has been extremely outspoken about boards that give their CEOs a rubber stamp. During the time George was CEO of Medtronic, his board once voted 11–1 to move forward with a proposed acquisition. Most CEOs would be overjoyed with this kind of resounding approval for an acquisition, but not George. He identified with the lone "no" vote, called the dissenter over the weekend, and asked him to go through, in detail, his objections. He knew that for someone to have the courage to be the lone dissenting voice, the person must have had some pretty good reasons. After George had heard all the arguments, he came to agree with the dissenter and the deal was called off. George did not lead simply for the sake of crossing the finish line and winning. He wanted to know what he and his people were winning—and if in fact they were winning. It's a case of substance over and above success.

Success comes and goes; but substantive decisions and actions are remembered . . . certainly by the individuals affected and, no surprise, by the leader who makes them. That's how a good night's sleep becomes an obtainable possibility.

Corporate leaders and investment analysts who have deliberately lied and stolen from their shareholders are now in the process of being publicly prosecuted; they are examples of American industry doing a good housecleaning. Board governance is changing rapidly as well. The new watchword in governance is *generative governing*, which is a more involved kind of board supervision, strategic and vigilant simultaneously. I'm hopeful about this trend, but it's going to take a long time to see it fully bear fruit. It's going to take baby boomers and Millennials and Generations X and Y demanding improved board performance. Having principles is not only the bedrock of leadership, it must become tantamount to increased profitability—the number-one sought-after quality in the global marketplace.

INTEGRITY

*Every action you take is a reflection
of your personal character.*

As the former head of pharmaceuticals for Bayer in the United States, Karen Dawes is a person who was called upon to show her store of integrity. During the 2001 anthrax scare, which occurred within days of the World Trade Center attacks, Cipro, a Bayer product, was one of the only antibiotics able to treat the anthrax bacteria, and that fact placed Dawes and her company in the national spotlight.

For those of us who have forgotten the ugly and frightening

details of that time, let me replay the scene for you. A man dies in Florida, his death attributed to a letter he opened that contained anthrax spores. An envelope containing anthrax is sent to former Senate minority leader Tom Daschle, causing the entire U.S. House of Representatives and Senate to be shut down so both chambers can be fumigated. People are advised not to open their mail unless they know exactly whom it is from. The nightly news is explaining to us what kinds of envelopes may be suspicious. Postal workers want protection. Post offices start irradiating our mail, slowing deliveries. Everyone wants medical protection from this deadly poison. Who manufactures one of the only antibiotics on the market proven to work against anthrax? Bayer does. It's Dawes's drug, Cipro.

The temptation for Bayer was to view the crisis opportunistically given the withdrawal of its blockbuster cholesterol-lowering drug, Baycol. But when a crisis like this is presented, leaders have a choice. And Bayer and Karen Dawes took the high road. Dawes told the class some things about September 11, 2001, and the response to the anthrax crisis that most people weren't aware of. On 9/11, one of the first things the government did was test the air in New York to see if there was evidence of anthrax. As it turned out, there was not. Said Dawes:

> "But we started thinking, as did everybody else, we're vulnerable. So we proactively at that point started to look at production capabilities for Cipro. Also on that day, we took Cipro from our distribution center in Connecticut and delivered it to New York hospitals. Ours were some of the few vehicles that were allowed to get over the bridges so that we could make sure that the hospitals had Cipro if they needed it. We thought at that point that as far as we were concerned the situation was under control, but it wasn't."

Not by a long shot. Anthrax soon became the number-one media story. The government wanted to have on hand additional supplies of Cipro in big numbers. It wanted 95 million tablets in government hands by the end of 2001, and Bayer took on that request and went into overdrive to make it happen. The first thing Bayer did, recalled Dawes, was put its wholesalers on notice that the government was their first priority and other requests would have to come second. Next, Bayer donated Cipro to the front lines—two million tablets to postal workers and anyone else charged with entering buildings threatened by anthrax. The company also forged a supply agreement with the U.S. government. Bayer and Karen Dawes acted for the purpose of long-term credibility and integrity.

Crisis situations bring tensions and headaches and exhaustion. But leaders who shepherd a company through a crisis also experience the often once-in-a-lifetime opportunity to discover the meaning of putting their principles into practice. And though Dawes's example is an extreme one, everybody makes daily choices to act on their principles or not to.

VULNERABILITY

Be human with your people. If you're honest with them, they'll love you for your faults as much as your strengths.

Without doubt, great leaders have feet of clay like the rest of us; but they must have the integrity to admit those flaws openly and be prepared to make the wrongs right, even if it costs them. If a leader can show her followers that she can admit mistakes, make them right, and move on, imagine the empowerment that gives the people in the front lines to take risks, make mistakes, admit them, change, and grow. It takes courage, mixed with a good dose of humility and self-esteem, to admit mistakes. We're conditioned very early on to believe that people won't like us if we're flawed. Leadership is so hard because it cuts against the grain of comfortable societal conditioning. The practice of *principles* is the ability to admit mistakes over and over again, air them, struggle to make them right, and move forward. When a leader can do that, she will have loyal followers—because it proves she's human, just like the rest of us.

There are those times when leaders do not do the right thing. They will make an impulsive decision, omit letting colleagues know of decisions, decline feedback, embarrass a colleague publicly, or hire an unqualified old friend. These things happen. Leaders must get to a place where they can say they're sorry (publicly, if necessary) and then take the necessary steps to right their wrongs.

Something I've learned over the years, and that I've tried to pass on to my direct reports, is that you should apologize and say when you've made a mistake. I've told some of my managers to practice saying it in the mirror every day. I can tell you, this was not a skill that came easily to me, but it's been one of the most important I've developed in trying to lead. It brings humility and humanity to the process. Even flexibility. If you choose to lead, be assured that you will make mistakes, that you may at times hurt your own and your organization's credibility. The good news, however, is that most of the time you will be able to make a correction, even though there may be a penalty attached to it.

Young people today inherently distrust the illusion of perfection. I think it's probably why so many people are riveted to television programs like *Survivor* and *The Apprentice*—where bad deeds occur in every show. We are imperfect people working for imperfect institutions—we all know this intuitively. If you want people to willingly follow you, leaders have to be honest about who they are and the mistakes they make.

ACCOUNTABILITY

Take personal responsibility for problems that arise in your organization, and take the appropriate measures to fix the problems.

Greg Young used to run the Fenwal Laboratories division at Baxter, which at the time was a large healthcare conglomerate that manufactured medical devices. Young is a leader who is forthright about his own mistakes and always held Baxter to that same standard of transparency.

Like Karen Dawes, Greg Young's integrity and credibility really had a chance to shine during his company's very public crisis in March 2003. The issue was the blood bags that Baxter manufactures. The American Red Cross, Baxter's major client, notified the company that the Red Cross blood bank in Atlanta had discovered white particulate matter in some of the blood bags Baxter supplied.

Young didn't try to make excuses or attribute the problem to cold temperatures or some other naturally occurring phenomenon that he believed to be the cause—he didn't equivocate at all. He listened to his customer's concerns thoughtfully and asked that they ship the bags back to Baxter's quality control group in Chicago for study. It turned out that no fault with the blood bags was found. Young and his management team at Baxter never came out on the defensive, despite the American Red Cross going to the media before getting the test results that cleared Baxter. Instead, he and his team worked to solve the problem the Red Cross was reporting, and then they applied themselves to figure out a means to permanently correct it.

After they got through with the immediate crisis, Young made sure that Baxter commissioned an independent study, conducted by some of the country's best blood transfusion experts, to look into the source of the problem. Baxter's product was proven perfectly safe, but that's not the point. The point is that Young didn't lay blame or obfuscate. As a leader he took on the responsibility to solve his customer's problem and stayed on top of the issue, 24/7, until it was resolved. Here's an instance where credibility is almost synonymous with accountability. Whether you made a mistake or didn't, recognize others are anxious and need answers. Help to regain confidence, make it right, and move forward.

Greg Young's credo is leadership is not about being right; it's about doing the right thing. It wasn't about Baxter looking good—it was about Baxter doing right. Leaders work to fix a problem regardless of what or who caused it. Jeff Rich calls this practice of fixing a problem without laying blame the "who shot John modality" and says it saves his company time and money every day. The thinking goes like this: If John comes in with a bullet wound, you don't start taking DNA samples, determining the trajectory of the bullet, or tracking down the killer . . . you do nothing else but try and save John's life. If you try to work through the problem by weighing and analyzing all the details, John will simply bleed to death. What Rich is saying, plain and simple, is to do what Greg Young did. If you see a problem, fix it. Don't probe and second-guess the causes. Just get in there and do the right thing! Later, when the bleeding stops and things stabilize, an analysis of cause is appropriate, but not in the moment of crisis.

Greg Young insists on his people being doers, not simply reporters. One discomforting thing he learned during the difficult time at Baxter was that he had several top people who reported

Jon:

As Dad and I were talking on our walk about dealing with crisis, something funny happened. I said I thought the "who shot John" idea was of Buddhist origin. At that, Dad said, "What do you mean, that's Buddhist? That's business." And my rejoinder? "Buddhist business, then." And we went on like that for a while, like Abbott and Costello, trudging up the mountain, laughing up a metaphorical storm.

The story, told by Buddha about 2,500 years ago, goes like this: There is a man with an arrow through his chest. The trajectory of the arrow, or who slung it or made it, is not the point. Buddha said the only objective was to practice the compassion of relieving the suffering of the one who has been struck. Save John, save the victim of the arrow, save the company from ruin . . . and do it with all the utmost steadfastness, attention, and integrity you can muster, no matter the consequences.

problems as if they were in a newsroom—factually, unemotionally, passively. Young recognized he didn't need people just to report the problems; he needed people with the integrity to work toward a fair solution and not quit until one was found and put into practice.

Father Joseph O'Hare, the now former president of Fordham University and its head when I started the Leadership Forum, stressed to the MBAs the importance of accountability in the academic context as well. Recalling his first year as university president and his first roundtable meeting with twenty-eight other presidents of the country's Jesuit colleges, O'Hare remembers a surprising lack of attention to accountability. "My first exposure to [the] occupational hazard of being a university president was this temptation toward presidential puffery. You're always telling people how good things are."

O'Hare said he discovered right then and there the powerful question raised in Steven B. Sample's book, *The Contrarian's Guide to Leadership.* In O'Hare's words, "Do you want to *be* president, or do you want to *do* president? If you simply want to be president and enjoy all the pomp and circumstance of it, then soon you're irrelevant. On the other hand, if you want to do the task and make the hard choices, be open about mistakes, conflicts, and difficulties, and show you care about fixing them, you're relevant." O'Hare was advocating that such relevance requires sizing up the situation of your organization honestly and tackling the tough issues head-on.

STEADFASTNESS

Show your courage. Demonstrate honesty in all situations—even when the consequences mean financial loss or a blow to your position.

Practicing principles is something you enact within the messy context of a real circumstance. Bill Toppeta, president of MetLife International, found that out quickly in Indonesia. In a "town hall" meeting there, a woman stood up and asked if the company permitted managers to take direct reports as mistresses. Toppeta said no, that was not okay. Some people objected and told Toppeta that he was trying to impose American values on a company of Indonesian culture where there is a very permissive attitude about these things. He responded that it had nothing to do with American morality,

which he would never impose. He said the reasons were very pragmatic and came down to performance issues:

> "By definition, for a manager to be credible he/she must have
> two things: She/he must be objective when judging the perfor-
> mance of direct reports, and he/she must be *perceived* as objective
> by all. Now, if a manager is sleeping with a direct report, he/she
> cannot be objective when it comes to rating that direct report's
> work performance. This is not a morality issue; it is a best busi-
> ness practice issue. And here at MetLife, our culture is about best
> business practice, and that culture transcends anything else."

As Toppeta demonstrates, it is essential for leaders to be able to
take a stand on their principles and communicate them clearly to
their people. This is why his response is so important to understand—the culture of the company's principles transcends the local
culture when the two are in conflict. Having principles often means
having to say "no."

On the personal level, saying no is often the last thing we are
trained to do in pursuit of our business goals. When I was younger,
business was like a basic training obstacle course. You couldn't wait
to climb over the next wall, hop through the tires, and jump over
the muddy water. You move when they tell you to move. All you
see is the finish line. It becomes all about getting there no matter
what stands in your way. If you can't scale the wall, go through it.
Embracing this attitude is how I (and many of my generation)
moved from being a corporate manager to chairman. I stayed at my
last CEO job for a decade and a half because I never took my foot
off the gas. I laced up my sneakers every day and worked to overcome the obstacles and hazards that were thrown in front of me.

To me, then, Vince Lombardi got it right when he said, "Winning isn't everything, it's the only thing." But an experience I went

through not too long ago helped me to revise my perspective a bit on attacking the obstacle course.

Discover Your "No" Principle

I had just walked into one of the most beautiful office lobbies in Manhattan. Before making my way to the elevators, the impeccably tailored security guard politely noted my laptop and indicated that I needed to show it to him. He handled it with a gentleness I have yet to see in an airport. In the marble-floored elevator I watched the numbers quickly shoot up to forty-three. Stepping off the elevator I was greeted by my host and led into an oak-paneled boardroom. A beautifully catered lunch was on the table and my host was pouring me a Perrier. This was old school. No women, no minorities, no one under fifty, just an old-time board of directors with a taste for their own importance.

The view from the windows was spectacular—the best in the city. This is the sort of boardroom you imagine exists, but aren't quite sure. You sense that joining the occupants of this place translates to immediately becoming part of an inner circle.

The field green salad sat perfectly on my oversize white plate. The white cloth napkin was spread across my lap, when my host began making small talk. The CEO was a colleague and friend and had proposed me for the board. This was no interview, it was a lunch among colleagues of equal stature and power . . . or so I thought.

Just as I was beginning to relax, one of the directors began chiding me and grilling me as to the weight and nature of my potential board contributions. This gentleman was a personality I recognized from one of television's talking-head news shows. He loved to hear himself talk, and it seemed he had a script in front of him now. He was quite enjoying giving me a stress interview and listening very little to my answers and differences in opinion. His celebrity status sufficiently intimidated the other directors, who sat by as he worked his way into a rant.

I had a couple of choices at this point. My usual retort was to do combat with such an individual and put him in his place with my knowledge of the pharmaceutical industry and my confidence in my own record of performance—either this person was a water hazard or a wall, and I would go around him or over him. While I sat there contemplating what I would say when he finally turned off his mouth, a brand-new thought came over me, one I had never before considered . . . I could just leave.

After being in business for forty years, hopefully your instincts tell you which people are open to new ideas, which like to hear themselves talk, and which just grow their egos, not their companies. You also get instincts about the culture of a company and whether innovation is welcomed. I took a good look around me, felt the weight of the Waterford crystal glass in my hand, set it down onto the slate coaster resting on the antique mahogany conference table, and observed myself rising from my chair. I couldn't believe what I was doing. Where was the old fighter? The Lombardi protégé trained to win at all costs?

Standing up straight with my chair pushed in and my jacket buttoned, I smiled and said something like, "Being on a board is an awful lot of work. I believe in what this company can be and I want it to thrive, and that's why I'm here; but my time is valuable to me and I'd prefer not to spend it with people I don't enjoy being with. I'm not enjoying this now and I doubt I would in the future." And then I did something I never had before. I turned and walked out. The CEO met me at the elevator a few minutes later, apologized and beseeched me to reconsider. I patted him on the back, thanked him, and left.

I made my way out of the lobby and onto those wonderfully

alive New York City midtown streets. I spotted a cigar shop. I lit up on the corner of Madison and 46th Street, amidst the energy of the real life going on around me. After all those years on the obstacle course, I thought to myself, maybe I'm finally learning the most difficult lesson of all—there are times that leaders choose not to play the game.

Smoking my cigar while trying to process what it was I had just done and what the implications would be, a teenager in hip-hop clothes walked by. "Got the time, chief?" he asked. I stuck out my hand and showed him my watch face and then smiled at the irony of it all. "Only for meaningful things," I answered. Saying "no" never felt so liberating. For me, in that moment, holding fast to what I knew was the right thing was far sweeter than achieving any external reward. It's hard to know this when you're younger . . . everything is pushing you to succeed. But success without principles is empty. Had I accepted that board position, I would have been handsomely compensated and I may have appeared more outwardly successful in some circles, but I wouldn't have felt good about myself in my gut. Let's face it—your gut doesn't care about outward appearances.

Courage Has Consequences

To do what you know is right, but that you suspect others might not understand, takes courage. There is no better recent example of this then General Eric Shinseki, former U.S. Army Chief of Staff. On February 25, 2003, while testifying before the Senate Armed Services Committee regarding the war in Iraq, he was asked how many troops he thought would be needed.

After a thirty-eight-year distinguished military career, a tour in Vietnam, service as commander of the U.S. Army and NATO in Europe as well as Bosnia, Shinseki felt no need to pull punches. He told Senator Carl Levin that several hundreds of thousands of troops would be required. Shinseki made his statements at the exact time his boss, Secretary of Defense Donald Rumsfeld, was working diligently to convince Congress that the Iraq war would require only a limited number of ground forces. After Shinseki's comments were made public, Rumsfeld and his deputy, Paul Wolfowitz, disparaged him. Wolfowitz called Shinseki's comments "wildly off the mark." Despite the personal and professional consequences, Shinseki never blinked. Besides being the recipient of verbal attacks in the press, Shinseki also had to withstand the unprecedented fact that his successor was named a full fourteen months before the end of his term. But intimidation and attempts at humiliation never stopped Shinseki from standing on his principles. He never recanted what he originally told the Senate; he remained humbly steadfast.

The expedient thing to do is to please the boss and to move on—to go with the flow of what those in power want to see executed. But Shinseki couldn't do that. He never allowed himself to become a yes-man, despite his involvement in a profession known for taking orders. In the end, for General Shinseki, being a soldier meant standing up and speaking up for the benefit of his troops' safety and security. Did he pay a short-term price of intense discomfort and unpleasantness? He did! But for a guy who lost a foot in Vietnam, he knew all about real discomfort. Shinseki refused to succumb to what Bill George of Medtronic calls *short termitis,* and instead made a decision to speak and act from his principles— however politically unpopular. Shinseki, a hero to all who know him or of him, recognized that as politics drift and change, principles do not. Remaining steadfast is a long-term proposition. The rewards don't come swiftly, lavishly, and hardly ever publicly. But in the days that follow the moment of truth when you acted in accord with your principles, the rewards come—your mirror holds a face you can look at with respect.

Jonathon's Perspective

It is easier to fight for one's principles than to live up to them.
—ALFRED ADLER

I think most people think of principles as fixed in stone. But even here, there is the necessity of flexibility. The respected American Zen teacher Steve Hagen illustrates this in a story about a Nazi S.S. guard whose job is going house to house in a Gentile neighborhood looking for Jews. Hagen points out if we hold German philosopher Immanuel Kant's categorical imperative to be law, then if asked if you are hiding any Jews, the person must tell the truth. But if the person lies to the Nazi at the door and answers no, then the hiding Jewish family would be safe to live another day. Kant never accounted for such an irrational situation where someone would be forced to lie to do the right thing.

The point is that without flexibility and awareness as to what is the right thing, we run the risk of living our principles the way robots do—doing something because we were programmed rather than listening to our conscience. So my dad has it right when he talks about principles as an active practice, something that we need to constantly consider.

Greg Young was put in a situation where he was called on to fulfill his company's duty to serve the public health without question and take responsibility for a situation he didn't cause, and to extend his best effort to come up with a resolution. In the situation Young was in, he did what was principled by taking it on the chin and working through the problem without defensiveness.

And what about loyalty? If you're a soldier in the army, the general rule is that you take orders from the top and carry them out without question; it is how things get done. That's why the example of General Shinseki is so interesting. Here we have the top soldier in the U.S. Army, the chief of staff, breaking the rule about loyalty and publicly opposing the judgment of the highest ranks, even the commander-in-chief, and stating what he believed to be true: U.S. troop strength in Iraq was undermanned.

For Shinseki, to be a "good soldier" meant being in touch with the needs of the troops, serving and listening to the ones on the bottom, not blindly heeding the opinion of his superiors. The point is that loyalty or personal responsibility on their own are not a good thing or a bad thing . . . they are porous concepts. What gives them their gravitas is the context. This is why we advocate thinking about the word *principles* as an action verb and not just a noun. Principles are figured out every day by thinking people walking into situations that have never happened before. There is no formula.

This is why leadership will remain forever mysterious. Because in the end you can't pin it down. You can't write down the formula of what makes a leader. What's at issue here is the context in which it is practiced.

It seems to me that as soon as you think you have your principles figured out, life goes and throws you a curve. My peers and I have to use our brains and our creative capacity to make choices about how to live our lives. We don't trust a rulebook for behavior. Rules and prescriptions don't suggest trust—they suggest control. Great leaders are such because they do the unexpected, and they are flexible enough to give a situation exactly what it requires. Great leaders never rely solely on their rulebook; they are mindful that life and work is an open book with no definitive and absolute conclusion.

In his treatise, *Walking*, Henry David Thoreau wrote:

> What is it that makes it so hard sometimes to determine whither we will walk? I believe that there is a subtle magnetism in Nature, which, if we unconsciously yield to it, will direct us aright. It is

not indifferent to us which way we walk. There is a right way; but we are very liable from heedlessness and stupidity to take the wrong one.

Walking was central to us in writing this book. The activity on its own nurtures body and soul, but the metaphor embedded in the activity is also significant. How do we choose to walk through this world? Which direction do we take when confronted with a choice? Do we follow Robert Frost's poetry and take the road less traveled by—thereby doing that thing that makes all the difference in our lives—or do we take the safe, well-worn path? To live our principles means we have to make tough choices. Thoreau claimed that we know what the right direction is—we just have to "yield to it."

When we listen closely we can hear Thoreau's "it" deep in our gut. But listening closely and yielding to nature requires us to say no to the temptations of ego. It means we will walk the way of turning down compensation if it is unethical, we will walk away from accolades if the credit belongs to others, and we will walk straight into trouble if it means being accountable for our mistakes. Our gut knows the way to a principled life, and when we go against it, we can feel the tension and stress in our bodies and minds.

I think about my dad standing up and walking out of that posh boardroom when he saw there something that conflicted with his principles. He called me from the street right afterward and I remember hearing the joy in his voice that day. He had just given up a good chunk of money and a modicum of prestige, and he never felt better because his gut was happy. Leaders know how choices live on in memory long after the temptation has passed. Whether one gets caught doing the wrong thing is irrelevant—going against your principles just feels bad, and money and titles can't ever make that feeling go away.

PRINCIPLES

Checklist for Leaders

Practice/Activity

❑ Credibility

Be honest with and thoughtful of your people. Admit mistakes readily.

❑ Integrity

Every action you take is a reflection of your personal character.

❑ Vulnerability

Be human with your people. If you're honest with them, they'll love you for your faults as much as your strengths.

❑ Accountability

Take personal responsibility for problems that arise in your organization, and take the appropriate measures to fix the problems.

❑ Steadfastness

Show your courage. Demonstrate honesty in all situations—even when the consequences mean financial loss or a blow to your position.

CHAPTER 9

PRACTICE

It Never Stops

You can't talk yourself out of problems that you behave your way into.
—STEPHEN COVEY

For the last leg of our North Carolina walk, Jon was taking me on a long hike up to Shining Rock. We would follow the Art Loeb trail on what Jon explained was one of the most unique terrains in the Blue Ridge Mountains. Here in North Carolina and Tennessee, the ridge is generally covered in green foliage. To get a view of how high up you are and how massive the mountain is across, you have to find an overlook. They don't show up often on these trails, so for the most part you are slogging through a dense canopy of trees.

Shining Rock is vastly different. You walk on rock for the most part and can see the wide open mountains on both sides of you. The wind rings in your ear, the sky above you is available and close at hand, and the sensations of being on a mountain are unmistakable. For a long time on the way up, I couldn't say a word, couldn't believe the beauty of it; I just had to breathe it in.

About halfway up, we turned on our wireless recording equipment and started talking about the subject of this chapter, practice.

After several hours, having what we thought was the most insightful conversation to date, we checked the tapes to see how they were recording. All we could hear was the whistling of the wind. I was very put out. Days later, after sending the tapes to a special transcription service to see if they could extract anything coherent, I finally started to realize the teaching in that beautiful scene that enveloped us. Words do flutter in the wind and drift off—actions stay. Walking on the open edge of the mountain to Shining Rock was the essence of this trip. Same goes for leadership practice—your actions are remembered and drawn upon; words are quickly forgotten. You can't talk your way into Carnegie Hall—you have to practice, practice, practice. And though the words spoken on the way to Shining Rock are gone forever, we hope that the intention behind them found their way into what we later recorded and now bring to you.

It all comes down to practice. Everything we have spoken of in the course of this book requires practice; it is the staple of all leadership. We begin with it and come back to it again and again. It can never be a goal because it is the way—the path itself. Practice transforms a person—it makes his mind and body relate to the world in a new way. This is true for a dancer, a musician, an athlete, a physicist, and it is true for a leader. We practice not simply for a goal—we practice because we love the discipline to which we have given ourselves over. To practice is to live and work as though there were no beginning, middle, or end to a goal. When you practice "practice," all that exists is the duty to give every moment all of your effort, holding nothing in reserve.

To lead, you must love it. The love will get you through those extremely difficult and unrewarding days. Leaders work at their craft. They don't coast. They don't take their skills as a given. They are driven to improve so they can help others to improve. Leaders hold nothing back—all of their practice is for the sake of inspiring and moving their followers forward on their own paths. A leader takes nothing for granted—she mixes the ingredient of practice into every recipe and, without it, she knows nothing will ever come out right.

All the leaders I interview and invite to the Fordham Leadership Forum I choose not because they are famous or successful in the eyes of a stock analyst, but because in them exists the duty to give *all* of their effort; nothing is held aside. This is the message I want to communicate to my students and to you.

Of all the leadership Ps, practice takes the most resolve. There always will be difficult times. There will always be an enticement, an issue at home, at work, with friends, that can easily distract you from accomplishing your goals. It takes tremendous effort not to indulge distractions. Practice is not an inborn skill; it's a habit. And that's good news for you hard workers who were never able to get by on inborn talent and charm. With many of the Ps—particularly I think of passion and purpose—a person can get very excited about the emotion behind them if it feels good. But what do you do when it doesn't feel good? What do you do when you don't feel passion or your purpose is not working out? This is a key question you have to ask yourself. The answer is what separates people who are leaders from people who are not.

Leaders are human beings with families, friends, and all the trappings that come with that; yet they're also looked up to. This fact has to be reconciled and acknowledged head on. They may employ few or many—10,000, 20,000, or in the case of Bill Toppeta, 47,000 people—and they are able to get through the issues and distractions and continue to lead and continue to further their vision, I believe, by clinging to these Ps. They practice them all the time. They don't have it perfect, ever. They just work the hardest at it. Leadership is labor-intensive.

Thomas Von Essen talked about that—the work of just getting

up every day to face reality regardless of what you are presented with, just doing your best, just doing the job. It's about developing a habit of work that encourages you to get up and do your job every day, regardless of circumstances.

I don't know exactly how people develop this capability. Clearly though, some people develop it and others don't. It's part of the leadership mystery. Some get thrown off the track and don't persevere. They feel a sense of purpose one day, and the next they don't know how to get back on track.

If you don't have a method of practice—if you don't have a sense that no matter what happens, you're going to simply stay in the moment of the work at hand—it's not hard to get thrown off. Smart mountain climbers always make sure they're tied off when they're working their way up a steep grade. If a big wind comes, a tree falls, or an avalanche hits, at least they have the rope as security to help them stay where they are. Practicing the Ps daily is a way of tying yourself off on the leadership mountain. The rope helps pull us up, but even more important, it keeps us from falling off.

When the difficulties come and you've made it a habit to practice "practice," you have in your bag an answer. You have a tested response to overcome the challenges. As Raul Cesan, the former president of Schering-Plough, told the Forum: "Every individual is the entrepreneur of their own job." No one can control all the things going on in the world; it's too random. With practice you can say to yourself, here in this industry, in this field, in this job, in this unit, is where I can take some control and change lives. You make decisions, your organization grows, you fill a societal need. That's practice, and it creates a sense of meaning and a sense of direct cause and effect.

To lead people is the greatest challenge in existence because it is truly not about managing resources, it is about understanding the human condition. At their heart, people want a practice. They want something in their lives that they know they can do and achieve, even if they don't exactly know what that something is. Leaders have to give it to them; they have to give their people a place of their own where they can make a difference.

One other thing is the importance of having a community of practice at work. Jeff Rich told us at ACS, the thing they practice is to head off little mistakes because they can turn into big costly mistakes if they're not dealt with early. Rich is practice-minded because he knows ACS will prosper if there is a sense of shared common practice.

In the end, as far as leadership is concerned, all we really have is practice. There is only the doing from moment to moment. There is no final arrival at Destination Leadership. As soon as you think you have arrived and you stop practicing, you're a goner. Think Michael Jordan here. No layups in the yard, no layups in the game. We have to watch ourselves closely here—never underestimate the human tendency to feel that something is finished. Leadership doesn't have a finishing point, game over; it is a practice to commit to and live.

Some people who don't know me that well ask me when I will retire. I tell them never. I know that the minute I retire, I run the risk of thinking there is nothing more to practice. You can retire from a position or from a company, but not from the practice of leadership if you want to remain productive and interesting to those around you.

In this book's Prologue, I said I would try to tell you how you could practice "practice." Recent studies by neuroscientists show that neural connections in a professional musician's brain are different from those in an amateur who practices twice a week. Practice shows. The honed skill can be detected. The message here is that to become a professional at leadership, you need to practice to the point where the nine Ps become second nature.

For Wynton Marsalis to become a virtuoso trumpet player and one of the leading jazz musicians in the world, he had to give himself over to the practice of jazz. The same can be said for Michael Jordan in basketball, Tiger Woods in golf, and Meryl Streep in film—their art form is synonymous with who they are as people. Their lives have become a practice. Leadership is the same way, but be cautious about calling yourself a leader. Outstanding actors, painters, and sculptors are careful not to call themselves artists; they let other people do that.

That said, the leadership P known as practice comes down to this—*you must practice leadership,* which means all the Ps, simultaneously and integrally. You'll notice that this chapter doesn't include a list of five practices for you to follow. It's all about the total forty practices highlighted at the end of each of the previous chapters. You're going to need ability in every single one. I told you that this leadership P is the hard one. It's the nine-stranded rope you'll depend on for future success.

Jonathon's Perspective

> A student said to Master Ichu, "Please write for me something
> of great wisdom." Master Ichu picked up his brush and wrote
> one word: attention. The student said, "Is that all?"
> The master wrote: Attention attention.
> —Charlotte Joko Beck, *Everyday Zen*

The fact that the audiotape of our conversation at Shining Rock recorded only the howling wind brought home for me one thought: that life is bigger than our ideas about it. We had a conversation of tremendous clarity and superb vocalization of our thoughts. We were able to see forever. Then we wound up without a tangible thing to show for it. We were unproductive! A sacrilege in business, I know.

The natural world had upset our plans. Indian poet and philosopher Rabindranath Tagore wrote, "In my life's garden, my wealth has been of the shadows and lights that are never gathered and stored." Our words blowing off the wind allowed us to truly digest our talk (along with our lunch of tuna sandwiches on that cliff) and, of course, to feel the wind.

I began my comments with a quote from Charlotte Joko Beck, one of America's most clear interpreters of Zen practice. In her story, paying attention is the thing—we must pay attention to how we practice. If we go at it in a rote way, we will not get to the place we want to go with leadership. We have all known colleagues who arrive early to the meetings, take copious notes, and constantly ask the boss what they can do to advance. This is how a lot of people climb the ladder, get tenure, or push ahead to a higher position. I don't feel this is conducting a leader's practice. It is the proverbial way we have been conditioned to "play the game." Sometimes the harder we work at becoming a leader, the less destined we are to achieve it.

A student at the monastery says to the teacher, "Master, if I practice very hard, how long will it take me to achieve enlightenment?" The master replies, "Ten years," and begins to walk off. The student persists: "But how about if I practice very, very hard?" The master looks him over and replies, "Twenty years." The master picks up his broom and starts to sweep the entryway. The stupefied student continues in the same vein. "What if I practice day and night without ceasing?" "Thirty years." the master answers.

In the Zen story, as the master saw the new student's growing sense of urgency with achieving enlightenment, the master knew the path would be that much harder for him—because enlightenment is not an end, it is a way. Leadership too is not an end; it is a way to be in the world.

The caveat here is these practices can't be grasped immediately and put in place overnight so you come out the other side with the stamp of LEADER across your forehead. Our culture loves anything fast, but authenticity takes time. It ripens with age. It takes a while for an acorn to become an oak tree, and such a miracle cannot be rushed. Without soil, water, sun, nutrients, and time, nothing happens. The wisdom of the acorn is that it knows this intuitively—it doesn't pop its head out of the dirt every five minutes and say "How am I doing?" It just grows at its own pace all the way to maturity.

We learned from every leader we spoke with that these practices have to take root day by day and year by year. The best thing we can do is to settle into these practices—not look at them as a test to pass, but rather as a life to live. If you picked this book up hoping to get some more strategies to succeed in business, then you got your hands on the wrong book. I know some readers hope that we'll just sum it all up here and boil down the nine leadership Ps to a few simple "must live bys." There is no such gold at the end of this rainbow. Just keep growing like the acorn and, hopefully, that's what we'll keep doing too.

Paying attention to one's leadership practice is ultimately a spiritual discipline. It means coming back again and again to the same question: What does it mean for *me* to lead? This is the constant *koan,* and the answer will change according to where we are in our lives. Leaders are ultimately charged with creating a meaningful context for others to carry out their work. Such a position is a tremendous responsibility and requires vigilant attention to others.

To truly be a leader, in my mind, means that one approaches the work of taking care and extending compassion to others as the ultimate privilege. Dad and I are in agreement that practice is a way, not a means to an end. I have learned so much from watching my own Zen teacher, Teijo Munnich. She has been practicing *zazen* (meditation) for thirty years, sitting day after day. She begins her seated meditation at 6 A.M. and never misses it. What does this say to me? That an authentic practice is ultimately not something that one does, but something that one is. And when we can become our practice there is no separation from it—we simply embody it. And this embodiment happens not by magic and it does not take root once and for all—it is constantly regenerated and strengthened through daily effort.

CHAPTER 10

CODA

The Tenth P—Providence

Sometimes your purpose finds you and sometimes providence finds you and then you find your purpose. This is a P we can't control, except that it is here in all of our lives. Time and again over the course of listening to the Fordham speakers and conducting the one-on-one interviews, before too long and sometimes sheepishly, someone would bring up the subject. Of course, because Fordham is a religious institution, the idea of providence is not such a foreign one, even in the MBA program.

But it wasn't Father O'Hare or Father McShane, the two presidents of Fordham University, who brought up this P. It was actually Sherman Lewis, the former vice chairman of Lehman Brothers (who died before the publication of this book) who mentioned to the class that providence would be his choice for a tenth P. And then the subject came up again when we talked with Bob Essner, the chairman and CEO of Wyeth, a Fortune 100 company. So this tenth one's for you, Sherman and Bob.

Lewis grew up in a small factory town in Illinois. His father, his uncles, and all his friends worked in the local Anchor Hocking glass factory. Lewis planned to do the same. He already had picked out the Buick convertible he would buy after high school graduation and had plans to ask his high school sweetheart to marry him. But before all that happened, providence stepped in and he was awarded a Naval ROTC scholarship to Northwestern University. Yale wanted him, he told the class, but he chose Northwestern because it was close to home.

He told his father he was giving college a try reluctantly and only because of how much it meant to his dad, and but that he'd probably be back home in a semester to take the job in the glass factory, buy the Buick, and get married, just like he'd planned. The short of it: Lewis never went back. He discovered he had a love for numbers and financial strategy and a natural affinity for them both.

After graduation he was recruited for a job in the financial field. His employer offered to pay the tuition if Lewis would go for his MBA. Again, on a lark, he said, why not? Claiming he never knew his purpose in any sort of self-directed way even for years after, Lewis attributed his stellar career path to providence. By no plan of his own, Sherman Lewis found his gift.

Lewis went on to pioneer financial and commodities markets, including what has become one of the most exciting and profitable fields on Wall Street, mortgage-backed securities. Like so many of the leaders we came in contact with, he credited his good fortune to the fact that he followed something other than his original plan.

The other standout example of this P is Robert Essner. He joined Wyeth in 1989 and has spent the last sixteen years leading this formidable company and helping to nationally and internationally shape an industry. Essner has been in the pharmaceutical business for most of his adult life, and he has transformed large segments of it with his enlightened vision of business development and his long-standing commitment to corporate governance.

When I first met Essner years ago, I just assumed he always

knew that health care was the business for him. His unshakable passion and obvious purpose were sure signs that he never for a second doubted in which direction he would move in life. It could not have been further from the truth.

Like Sherman Lewis, Bob Essner hails from the Midwest. Born and raised in Akron, Ohio, he did his undergraduate work at the University of Miami in Oxford, Ohio. Essner was a history major and loved it. He thought he would go on to become a history professor and never imagined doing anything else. An A student, he went to the University of Chicago (not far from where Lewis studied at Northwestern) to pursue his PhD in history. He got as far as his master's degree when he began to hear rumors that the universities across the country were not doing much hiring. There seemed to be a glut of professors, especially history professors. Being a pragmatic Ohioan, he figured that he better have a backup plan for making a living. As his next move, he took a job in the pharmaceutical industry, figuring that as things cleared up in academia, he could still go back for his PhD and spend the rest of his career in the history department of a small liberal arts school.

But providence would not have it. It turned out that Essner found something in business that he could never find in history— the unknown of the present and future moment. As much as he loved history (he is still a buff), it did not compare with the excitement of weighing decisions about things that have not yet happened. The thrill of business yet-to-be, combined with the satisfaction of producing medications for those who need it most, gave Essner a joy in purpose he had never imagined. From the time he was a boy, Essner thought he would spend his life as a history teacher, but because of a poor job market, he found himself on the career path that he was truly meant to pursue. Providence.

There is an expression in Yiddish that says, "We make plans and God laughs." We don't always have knowledge about what's best for us. Sometimes those circumstances that we think are taking us off the track are exactly the ones that show us our purpose and change our lives forever.

As you work through the preceding nine Ps, we hope you will free yourself to enjoy the ride and let in the possibility it just might be the tenth P, providence, that brings up a whole new journey waiting for you.

Jonathon's Perspective

Chance is a nickname for providence.
—WILLIAM CAMDEN

First blush of that word *providence* brings up Calvinist notions of predestination, yet what Bob Essner and Sherman Lewis are talking about are the blessings of circumstantial accidents. The Dalai Lama tells us to remember that not getting what you want is sometimes a wonderful stroke of luck. After I got my MFA in playwriting, I wanted to be a full-time working playwright more than anything. I had won awards, had the support of mentors, and was being encouraged by British playwright Edward Bond, who, when I was living in Los Angeles, even wrote a letter of recommendation for me to win a playwriting fellowship at the Manhattan Theatre Club. I wanted it so badly I could taste it, but it didn't happen. At the time, my arrogance and idealism about the theater and my disdain for television kept me from joining the ranks of Los Angeles television writers.

So I left Los Angeles and, rather than move to New York City, I went to Asheville, North Carolina, sight unseen, based on the recommendation of someone I met at a playwriting conference. She spoke convincingly about the Blue Ridge Mountains and I was hooked. And for a time I had what felt like a perfect life. A little house we loved, a job that felt meaningful, and no agents or LA traffic. I remember feeling that I wish nothing would change. Then my son was born and suddenly there wasn't enough time, room, or money, and things had to change. I look back and feel so incredibly grateful for those changes that at the time felt so disconcerting. My son undoubtedly gave birth to me in ways I cannot express. Providence takes you to places you never planned for; the key is, how do you embrace that accidental chance with a sense of wonder?

The mark of a great leader, I think, is how well she can say yes to providence. What a lesson for a leader to get her head around! We love to plan in business—objectives, strategy, and tactics. I can feel my mouth water when I think of how nice it sometimes would be to feel in control of the situation, as if you're the one driving it. When we're upended, we're at once reminded, "Oh yeah, I don't drive this thing; best I can do is learn the gentle art of adaptation." Providence descends and we are called upon to accept, not to question, lament, or berate, but simply to adapt to the new situation with a sense of grace and then reconfigure as necessary.

Do I think my life is providential? Maybe. I do believe I also have a fair amount of free will. The truth is that as a result of my personal choices as well as the providential circumstances beyond my control, I'm living this reality now. I count my blessings.

EPILOGUE

What We Know Now That
We Didn't Know Then

FROM JONATHON

Pema Chödrön, the first ever Westerner to be ordained as a Tibetan Buddhist nun and the Abbot of Gampo Shasta Abbey in Nova Scotia, wrote a book titled *The Places That Scare You.* Her thesis is that the only way to fully grow and develop into the people we need to be is to go directly to those places that scare us.

I traveled 10,000 miles around the country on a Greyhound bus when I was twenty-one. I had only a backpack, a few books, little money, and a journal. I did odd jobs along the way, including day labor with drunks, drug addicts, and drifters. That didn't scare me. I worked the overnight shift in a gas station next to the George Washington Bridge in New York that was not well lit; there was a lot of cash on hand, but I refused to have a gun. That didn't scare me. I worked with homeless people and inside the ramshackle homes of people on the edge. That didn't scare me. I camped through the fall and early winter in the icy cold mountains of Montana and Wyoming and woke up with snow weighing down my tent. That didn't scare me. I lived in the Old City of Jerusalem during the winter and spring of 1996. Buses were blowing up all around me. That didn't scare me.

This project of walking and working on a book with my dad scared me. Family is that place in your life where the deepest love resides as well as the deepest hurts. When you visit that place intimately, you never know exactly what will come up. I feared the closeness we would embark upon as much as I longed for it. It's why I knew it was important and that once he asked me, nothing would stand in the way of doing it.

Before entering the world of business, I carried around a lot of prejudices inside my head. Prejudices that I didn't think mattered—which are the worst kind because they are born of self-righteous ignorance and arrogance. And they extend out everywhere—even to your loved ones. I thought it was right to be prejudiced against the "man (woman) in the gray flannel suit." I thought the corporate uniform they wore and the industries they served were not creative. I unconsciously felt that "they" were money driven, did not care about the environment, and did not value time with their children enough.

Getting into business myself and then digging deeply into my assumptions about it—through walking this walk and writing this book with Dad—made me realize how wrong I was. I have met incredibly innovative thinkers living lives rich with meaning who care deeply for the environment, their families, and their personal integrity. Some of them wear gray flannel suits and work in financial services, law, insurance, pharmaceuticals, and consumer marketing. My openness to alternative culture did not excuse my prejudice against the mainstream. Writing this book taught me how much we all need each other to move forward in building a better world. There are incredibly creative and powerful people who want to lead in ways that lift people up and bring them together. Any prejudice gets in the way. I've tried to make my own practice one in which I strive to let go of labels.

Pema Chödrön tells a story of a friend of hers on death row who transformed his life while in prison. She recounts how the man would watch TV with the volume turned off. He got interested in watching protests and marches. And whether the cause was the KKK or Greenpeace, he began to notice some commonalities of expression without listening to the words. He saw that when people were angry they looked the same. The content of what they said meant little compared to the expression on their faces that communicated hatred of those people on the "other side."

Did Dad and I grow closer from this project? In ways that I could not begin to put into words. Did we change? Absolutely. After what seemed like an eternity of trying to convince the other of our rightness, we learned to listen to each other. As Thoreau says, "It is never too late to give up your prejudices." Dad and I were lucky. It wasn't too late for us. It's not too late for you, either.

FROM SANDER

It's quite a thing to be able to take time out with your son when he is grown and a father himself. I don't think Jonathon ever understood what I did before, never knew why I cared so much and why building a legacy was important to me. And when you don't feel understood by your child, a major piece of your life is missing. Children often think that it is only they who need acceptance from us. But we need acceptance from them, too—we need to know that our namesakes respect us as people as much as they need us as parents.

Your children know you in ways that nobody else does. They know you this way because they watch you for a lifetime. They look for signs of anger, love, reassurance, and encouragement. Reading these signs teaches them how to survive and get what they need. They are also learning to imitate—learning how to cope with the daily functions of life. For a long time, I think you live with the fantasy that because of that early imitation, your children will be just like you. But this is never the case. At first that may seem like an insult, a rejection of all that you gave.

But in time, as you grow, you see that your children were never just imitating; they were experimenting until they found what worked for them. To have a son who is different from you, like my Jonathon is, is such a blessing because you have not just a son, but also a teacher. I find this also very true of my creative and talented daughter, Pamela. You realize you fathered not a "chip off the old block" but another block entirely. You realize that as a parent, you have the opportunity to give birth to a new world. You teach them and they teach you and together you both grow up into fuller people than you ever could have become on your own. This is a gift beyond reckoning.

In the end, parenting is the best model of leadership I know. We train our young ones so they can one day fly the coop and surpass us, so they may return and teach us things we never could have taught them. I taught Jon to ride a bike even though I never learned to ride one. I remember standing on Fletcher Court, the street he grew up on, feeling breathless as I watched him drift away on that red bike. "Don't look back, Jon!" I hollered. "Just pedal . . . pedal . . . and look forward!" And he did.

Jon says it's not too late for me—sometime soon he'll teach me to ride a bike—and that our next book will be a journey on bicycles through Asia. I can't wait.

APPENDIX A: RESOURCES

BOOKS ON LEADERSHIP

Adizes, Ichak. *Managing Corporate Lifecycles.* Paramus, NJ: Prentice Hall, 1999.

Barry, Douglas. *Wisdom for the Young CEO.* New York: Running Press Books, 2005.

Bennis, Warren. *An Invented Life: Reflections on Leadership and Change.* Reading, MA: Addison-Wesley, 1993.

———. *On Becoming a Leader.* Reading, MA: Addison-Wesley, 1989.

———. *Why Leaders Can't Lead: The Unconscious Conspiracy Continues.* San Francisco: Jossey-Bass, 1989.

Bennis, Warren, and Joan Goldsmith. *Learning to Lead: A Workbook on Becoming a Leader.* Reading, MA: Addison-Wesley, 1994.

Bennis, Warren, and Burt Nanus. *Leaders: The Strategies for Taking Charge.* New York: Harper and Row, 1985.

Bossidy, Larry, and Ram Charan. *Execution: The Discipline of Getting Things Done.* New York: Crown Business, 2002.

Buckingham, Marcus, and Curt Coffman. *First, Break All the Rules: What the World's Greatest Managers Do Differently.* New York: Simon & Schuster, 1999.

Cobbs, Price M., and Judith L. Turnock. *Cracking the Corporate Code: The Revealing Success Stories of 32 African-American Executives.* New York: AMACOM, 2003.

Collins, James C., and Jerry I. Porras. *Built to Last: Successful Habits of Visionary Companies.* New York: HarperBusiness, 1994.

Cooper, Robert K., and Aymen Sawaf. *Executive EQ: Emotional Intelligence in Leadership and Organizations.* New York: Penguin Putnam, 1997.

Covey, Stephen R. *Principle-Centered Leadership.* New York: Summit, 1991.

DePree, Max. *Leadership Is an Art.* New York: Doubleday, 1989.

Drucker, Peter F. *The Effective Executive.* New York: Harper and Row, 1967.

———. *The Essential Drucker: Selections from the Management Works of Peter F. Drucker.* New York: HarperBusiness, 2001.

Eccles, Robert G., and Nitin Nohria, with James D. Berkley. *Beyond the Hype: Rediscovering the Essence of Management.* Boston: Harvard Business School Press, 1992.

Goleman, Daniel. *Emotional Intelligence: Why It Can Matter More than IQ.* Toronto: Bantam, 1995.

———. *Working with Emotional Intelligence.* New York: Bantam, 1998.

Goleman, Daniel, Richard Boyatzis, and Annie McKee. *Primal Leadership: Realizing the Power of Emotional Intelligence.* Boston: Harvard Business School Press, 2002.

Greenleaf, Robert K. *Servant Leadership: A Journey into the Nature of Legitimate Power and Greatness.* New York: Paulist Press, 1977.

Hankin, Harriet. *The New Workforce: Five Sweeping Trends That Will Shape Your Company's Future.* New York: AMACOM, 2005.

Heider, John. *The Tao of Leadership: Leadership Strategies for a New Age.* Toronto: Bantam, 1986.

Katzenbach, Jon R. *Peak Performance: Aligning the Hearts and Minds of Your Employees.* Boston: Harvard Business School Press, 2000.

Kelley, Robert E. *How to Be a Star at Work: 9 Breakthrough Strategies You Need to Succeed.* Toronto: Random House, 1999.

Kotter, John P. *Leading Change.* Boston: Harvard Business School Press, 1996.

———. *Power and Influence: Beyond Formal Authority.* New York: The Free Press, 1985.

Kotter, John P., and James L. Heskett. *Corporate Culture and Performance.* New York: The Free Press, 1992.

Kouzes, James M., and Barry Z. Posner. *Credibility: How Leaders Gain and Lose It, Why People Demand It.* San Francisco: Jossey-Bass, 1993.

———. *The Leadership Challenge: How to Keep Getting Extraordinary Things Done in Organizations.* San Francisco: Jossey-Bass, 1995.

Mai, Robert and Alan Akerson. *The Leader As Communicator: Strategies and Tactics to Build Loyalty, Focus Effort, and Spark Creativity.* New York: AMACOM, 2003.

McHugh, Donald E. *Golf and the Game of Leadership: An 18-Hole Guide for Success in Business and in Life.* New York: AMACOM, 2004.

Nanus, Burt. *Visionary Leadership: Creating a Compelling Sense of Direction for Your Organization.* San Francisco: Jossey-Bass, 1992.

Peters, Tom. *The Pursuit of WOW! Every Person's Guide to Topsy-Turvy Times.* Toronto: Random House, 1994.

Peters, Tom, and Nancy Austin. *A Passion for Excellence: The Leadership Difference.* New York: Random House, 1985.

Peters, Thomas J., and Robert H. Waterman, Jr. *In Search of Excellence: Lessons from America's Best-Run Companies.* New York: Harper and Row, 1982.

Pitcher, Patricia. *Artists, Craftsmen, and Technocrats: The Dreams, Realities, and Illusions of Leadership.* Toronto: Stoddart Publishing, 1995.

Sample, Steven B. *The Contrarian's Guide to Leadership.* San Francisco: Jossey-Bass, 2002.

Seibert, Donald V., and William Proctor. *The Ethical Executive: A Top C.E.O.'s Program for Success with Integrity in the Corporate World.* New York: Simon & Schuster, 1984.

Seligman, Martin E. P. *Learned Optimism.* New York: Knopf, 1991.

Tulgan, Bruce. *Winning the Talent Wars.* New York: W. W. Norton, 2001.

Uldrich, Jack. *Soldier, Statesman, Peacemaker: Leadership Lessons from George C. Marshall.* New York: AMACOM, 2005.

Ulrich, David, Jack Zenger, and Norm Smallwood. *Results-Based Leadership.* Boston: Harvard Business School Press, 1999.

Walton, Sam. *Made in America: My Story.* New York: Bantam, 1993.

Welch, Jack. *Jack: Straight from the Gut.* New York: Warner Business, 2002.

Welch, Jack, with Suzy Welch. *Winning.* New York: HarperCollins Publishers, 2005.

Zemke, Ron, Claire Raines, and Bob Filipczak. *Generations at Work: Managing the Clash of Veterans, Boomers, Xers, and Nexters in Your Workplace.* New York: AMACOM, 2000.

BOOKS ON ZEN PRACTICE

Aitken, Robert. *Taking the Path of Zen.* New York: Farrar, Straus, and Giroux, 1982.

Beck, Charlotte Joko. *Everyday Zen,* ed. Steve Smith. San Francisco: Harper-Collins, 1989.

Chödrön, Pema. *Places that Scare You.* Boston: Shambhala Publications, 2002.

———. *When Things Fall Apart.* Boston: Shambhala Publications, 1996.

———. *The Wisdom of No Escape.* Boston: Shambhala Publications, 1991.

Hagen, Steve. *Buddhism Plain and Simple.* New York: Broadway Books, 1997.

Huber, Cheri. *The Fear Book.* Mountain View, Calif.: Keep It Simple Books, 1995.

Katigiri, Dainan. *You Have to Say Something.* Boston: Shambhala Publications, 1998.

APPENDIX B: ABOUT THE LEADERS DISCUSSED IN THIS BOOK

REBECCA ANDERSON

As founder and executive director of HandMade in America, Rebecca (Becky) Anderson coordinates more than fifteen major projects involving 3,500 citizens and over twenty partnerships with local, regional, and state organizations and institutions. In 2000, *U.S. News and World Report* named her one of America's top-ten visionaries for her work in community and civic development. In 2003, *Worth* magazine ranked HandMade in America one of the twenty-five best arts nonprofits in the United States, saying it provided "the biggest bang for your buck" and represented "the best of our country's culture."

Anderson has twenty-eight years of experience in economic and community development work. She serves as a leading consultant for heritage and cultural tourism, as well as economic development projects related to arts and crafts.

JEFF ARONIN

Jeffrey S. Aronin is the founder and president of Ovation Pharmaceuticals, Inc. Ovation is a fully integrated pharmaceutical company that develops, acquires, manufactures, and markets prescription drugs. One of the fastest-growing pharmaceutical companies in the United States, Ovation currently markets eleven drugs and has more pending. Since its founding in 2000, the company has doubled in size and revenues every year, with a goal of $200 million in revenues for 2006.

Before starting and running Ovation Pharmaceuticals, Aronin was chairman and CEO for two successful healthcare companies, RxMarketing and MedCare Technologies. In 2004, he was named one of *Crain's Chicago Business* "40 Most Influential People Under 40" and was inducted into the prestigious Chicago Entrepreneurship Hall of Fame. Aronin also received the American Porphyria Foundation 2004–2005 Partner of the Year Award and was named the 2004 Corporate Citizen of the Year by the Epilepsy Foundation of greater Chicago. Aronin sits on several business and philanthropic boards.

JOHN W. BARDO

John W. Bardo has been the chancellor of Western Carolina University (WCU) since 1995. Under his leadership, WCU has seen dramatic growth and a remarkable transformation. Bardo has created nine fully funded endowed professorships, raised more than $20 million for the endowment, and increased active research grants from $2.5 to almost $13 million. Enrollment is up to nearly 8,000 and is expected to increase to 10,200 by the year 2012.

Bardo previously taught at Wichita State University, College of Swanson in Wales, and Monarch University in Australia. He was dean of the school of liberal arts at Southwest Texas State University and, later, vice president for academic affairs at University of North Florida in Jacksonville.

His writings have appeared in more than seventy professional publications, and he is the author of two books. Bardo speaks widely about the importance of technology in education and the role of higher education in economic and community development.

NICOLAS BAZAN

Founder-director of the Louisiana State University (LSU) Neuroscience Center of Excellence, Dr. Nicolas Bazan leads faculty, postdoctoral fellows, and graduate students who are investigating brain and eye function and diseases. He is a Boyd Professor, the highest academic honor in the LSU system. Bazan also occupies the Ernest C. and Yvette C. Villere Endowed Chair for the Study of Retinal Degeneration and is a professor of ophthalmology, biochemistry and molecular biology, neurology, and neuroscience in the School of Medicine of the LSU Health Sciences Center in New Orleans.

Bazan has achieved international renown for his pioneering discoveries that have advanced understanding of retinitis pigmentosa and age-related macular degeneration. In addition, he has unraveled key events in the disease processes of stroke, epilepsy, Alzheimer's disease, head trauma, and pain.

Bazan holds eighteen patents and has received numerous professional awards, including honorary membership in the Royal Academies of Sciences and Medicine (Spain), the Jacob Javits Neuroscience Investigator Award from the National Institutes of

Health, the Endre Balazs 2000 Prize of the International Society for Eye Research, and an Elected Fellowship in the Royal College of Physicians of Ireland. Bazan has edited seventeen books and published more than 500 original articles. He is the editor-in-chief of *Molecular Neurobiology* and has been a member of the editorial boards of the following publications: *Journal of Biological Chemistry, Journal of Neurochemistry, Journal of Cerebral Blood Flow and Metabolism, Current Neurovascular Research, Recent Patent Reviews on CNS Drug Discovery, Handbook of Neurochemistry and Molecular Neurobiology, Journal of Neuroscience Research, Neurochemical Research, Proceedings of the Society for Experimental Biology and Medicine, Neurotoxicity Research, NeuroMolecular Medicine,* and *Cellular and Molecular Neurobiology.*

GERALD BELLE

Jerry Belle assumed the position of executive chairman of Merial Ltd. on November 1, 2004. Merial is an innovation-driven animal health company developing products to enhance the health, well-being, and performance of a wide range of animals. Merial employs approximately 6,000 people and operates in more than 150 countries worldwide. Its 2004 sales were in excess of $1.8 billion. Merial is a joint venture between Merck & Co., Inc. and Sanofi-Aventis, two of the world's largest human pharmaceutical companies.

Belle is the former president of Aventis, North America pharmaceuticals, where he was responsible for the company's activities in the United States and Canada. His career in pharmaceuticals and life sciences spans more than thirty-five years. In 1969, he joined Merrell-National Laboratories. After a tour of service in the United States Army, he returned to Merrell-National and continued a steady succession of positions of increasing responsibility in the industry, including the presidencies of Hoechst Marion Roussel Canada and Hoechst Marion Roussel North America, before becoming president of Aventis North America in 1999.

RAUL CESAN

Raul E. Cesan was elected to the board of directors of The New York Times Company in 1999. He is the founder and has served as the managing partner of the investment firm Commercial Worldwide LLC since 2001. Previously, he served as president and chief operating officer of the Schering-Plough Corporation from 1998 until 2001, culminating a twenty-four-year career at the company.

He joined Schering-Plough, which is engaged in the discovery, development, manufacturing, and marketing of pharmaceutical and healthcare products worldwide, in 1977 as director of finance and administration for the company's Latin America region. He subsequently held positions of increasing responsibility, including president of operations in Europe, the Middle East, and Africa, and was appointed president of Schering-Plough International in 1988. In 1992, he became president of Schering Laboratories, the U.S. pharmaceutical marketing arm, and in 1994, was named president of Schering-Plough Pharmaceuticals.

KAREN DAWES

Karen A. Dawes is the principal and founder of Knowledgeable Decisions, LLC, a consulting firm that specializes in launching new products and assisting emerging pharmaceutical companies with commercialization strategies. She has been responsible for the successful launch and marketing of products in the cardiovascular, metabolic, infectious disease, central nervous system (CNS), hematology/oncology, and women's and men's health areas, including five separate products that each exceeded $1 billion in sales. She is a member of the board of directors of Protein Design Labs, Inc. and Genaissance Pharmaceuticals. She is a frequent lecturer to academic and corporate audiences on pharmaceutical marketing.

Dawes has twenty years of commercial experience in the pharmaceutical industry, beginning with ten years as a marketing executive at Pfizer, Inc. She was vice president of commercial operations at Genetics Institute, Inc., and then senior vice president, global strategic marketing, at Wyeth. Before forming her own consulting company, Dawes was senior vice president, U.S. business group head, at Bayer Pharmaceuticals Corporation.

ROBERT ESSNER

Robert Essner, chairman, president, and chief executive officer, joined Wyeth (formerly American Home Products Corporation) in 1989 as senior vice president, sales and marketing, for Wyeth-Ayerst Laboratories. In 1991, he was appointed to the position of executive vice president for the company and, two years later, became president of Wyeth-Ayerst Laboratories, responsible for the domestic pharmaceutical business. In 1997, he was named president of Wyeth-Ayerst Global Pharmaceuticals. The same year, he was elected to the position of executive vice president and member of the board of directors, Wyeth. In 2000, he was elected president and chief operating officer. Essner became chief executive officer in May 2001 and chairman in January 2003.

Currently, Essner is chairman of the Children's Health Fund Corporate Council as well as a member of the Business Roundtable and Business Council. In addition, he is a member of the board of directors of Massachusetts Mutual Life Insurance Company and the board of trustees of Penn Medicine, the entity governing the University of Pennsylvania School of Medicine and the University of Pennsylvania Health System. Essner is past chairman of the Pharmaceutical Research and Manufacturers of America.

JOHN GLENN

On February 20, 1962, John Glenn rode into space and around the globe three times, becoming the first American to orbit the earth. Before joining NASA, Glenn was a distinguished fighter pilot in both WWII and Korea. He retired from the Marine Corps in 1965, after twenty-three years in the military, with over fifteen medals and awards, including the NASA Distinguished Service Medal and the Congressional Space Medal of Honor.

Glenn received a bachelor of science degree and honorary doctor of science degree in engineering from Muskingum College in Ohio, as well as honorary degrees from nine other colleges or universities. He spent ten years as a business executive and then, in 1974, was elected to the United States Senate, where he served from 1974 until his retirement in 1999.

In 1998, Glenn was invited to rejoin the space program he helped to create, as a member of the crew of the space shuttle *Discovery*. He accepted and became the oldest human ever to visit space. Shortly after, Glenn and his wife, Annie, founded the John

Glenn Institute for Public Service and Public Policy at Ohio State University. Through its programs, they seek to improve the quality of public service and encourage young people to pursue careers in government. The Glenns also serve as trustees of Muskingum College, their alma mater.

BILL GRAY

Bill Gray joined Ogilvy & Mather as an assistant account executive in 1978. Today, he is president of the New York agency and a member (since 1994) of the worldwide board. During Gray's tenure as president, the agency has been named Agency of the Year by both *Adweek* and *Advertising Age*. The New York office is the largest in the Ogilvy network.

Gray has worked with a broad range of domestic and global clients, most notably American Express, which he headed in the early 1990s. He has twice won the coveted David Ogilvy Award and has contributed to an array of campaigns that have won Cannes Lion, One Show Pencil, and numerous Effy awards.

Gray is very involved in industry as well as civic and cultural activities. He sits on the board of the 4As (the American Association of Advertising Agencies) and the Ad Council and is a member of the National Advertising Review Board. He is also currently chairman of the board of the American Red Cross of Greater New York and a trustee of both the New York Public Library and the National Corporate Theatre Fund. In his hometown of Southport, Connecticut, he is on the board of the Wakeman Boys and Girls Club.

FRANCES HESSELBEIN

Frances Hesselbein is the founder and chairman of the board of governors of the Leader to Leader Institute and former CEO of the Girl Scouts of America. She has been presented with numerous awards and honors, including the Presidential Medal of Freedom, the country's highest civilian honor, and the first Dwight D. Eisenhower National Security Series Award for her service with the U.S. Army. President Bill Clinton called her a "pioneer for women, diversity, and inclusion." Former President George H. W. Bush appointed her to two commissions on community service.

Hesselbein has been featured on the covers of *Newsweek* and *Savvy* magazines, as well as in an issue of *Fortune* and *Chief Executive* on leadership. *Fortune* cited her as the "Best Nonprofit Manager in America." She has been included in Who's Who in America, Who's Who in Finance and Industry, Who's Who of American Women, and Who's Who in the World. Hesselbein has received seventeen honorary degrees.

She serves on many nonprofit and private-sector corporate boards and is chairman of the national board of directors for the Volunteers of America. Hesselbein is editor-in-chief of the quarterly journal *Leader to Leader* and coeditor of the book of the same name, as well as numerous others. She is the author of *Hesselbein on Leadership,* published in 2002.

ARTHUR HILLER

Arthur Hiller is senior vice president of Millennium Pharmaceuticals, Inc. He joined the company as general manager in February

2001 in charge of the company's inflammatory disease drugs. A year later, he was named general manager, cardiovascular, where he led a cross-functional team responsible for implementing the overall strategic vision of Millennium's cardiovascular business. In August 2003, he became senior vice president, global strategic marketing, and ultimately senior vice president, cardiovascular sales and marketing, in February 2004. In addition to leading the sales and marketing team for INTEGRILIN, the company's flagship product, his functional responsibilities include new product marketing for the Millennium pipeline. Before joining Millennium, Hiller worked for Merck & Co.'s human health division as vice president, worldwide human health marketing, hospital products.

JAMIE HUYSMAN

Jamie Huysman is the executive director and cofounder of the Leeza Gibbons Memory Foundation, as well as a national speaker and private clinical psychologist. His dynamic career has spanned every facet of health care, from direct service to hospital administration to the position of corporate vice president.

While vice president of a national group of hospitals, he created and implemented the first public-private treatment initiative in Washington, D.C. Huysman then went on to work with the Office of National Drug Control Policy and with the Reverend Jesse Jackson's Rainbow Coalition. He has appeared on more than 100 nationally syndicated talk shows as a clinical expert and has had his own radio show in South Florida for several years. He continues to be profiled in hundreds of local, national, and international newspapers and magazines and has been interviewed internationally on television and radio. In 2002, the BBC coproduced a documentary about his work with TV Aftercare.

Huysman maintains two private practices and does clinical work with the Centers for Psychological Growth.

NANCY LUBLIN

Nancy Lublin is the CEO of Do Something, a nonprofit organization that provides inspiration and opportunities for young people to improve their communities. Before that, in 1996, she founded Dress for Success, an international nonprofit that helps low-income women make "tailored transitions" into the workforce. Originally created to provide interview suits to women seeking employment, Dress for Success has since expanded to include job retention help and career development programs. Since its inception, Dress for Success has served more than 100,000 women in over seventy cities in four countries, and Lublin has been featured on television (*The Oprah Winfrey Show, 60 Minutes, Today,* CNN) and in *People, Reader's Digest,* and most major women's magazines. She has received various awards and honors including *Forbes* magazine's Trailblazer Award and *Ms.* magazine's Feminists for the Twenty-First Century Award. Lublin was the 2000 NYC Women's Commission Woman of the Year, and in 2001 she was Leadership America's keynote honoree.

Lublin is also a board member of the Nonprofit Coordinating Committee of New York and America's Charities.

CAM MARSTON

Consultant, author, and acclaimed speaker Cam Marston educates employers on managing, motivating, and retaining Generation X and Generation Y employees. Founder of Marston Communications in Charlotte, North Carolina, he has shared his insight with hundreds of organizations eager to make sense of the changing business landscape. His clients include General Electric, American Express, the Food Marketing Institute, Professional Convention Management Association (PCMA), and the U.S. Army.

Marston gives speeches throughout the United States and Canada and has traveled to Argentina and Australia to educate audiences on Generation X. He has appeared as a guest on several talk radio shows, been interviewed by *Entrepreneur* magazine, *Meetings & Conventions* magazine, the *Chicago Tribune,* and several other city papers and business journals. He chairs the Chapter Cities Committee for the Tulane Alumni Association; is a regular commentator on the Charlotte National Public Radio station, WFAE; and is involved with a number of civic groups in Charlotte.

Marston is the author of the upcoming self-published book, *Motivating the "What's in It for Me" Workforce: Managing Across the Generational Divide.*

REVEREND JOSEPH McSHANE

Joseph McShane became Fordham University's thirty-second president on July 1, 2003. Father McShane is also a trustee of St. Joseph's Preparatory School in Philadelphia, Loyola University in New Orleans, and the Association of Independent Colleges and Universities of Pennsylvania. He is a member of the executive committee of the Association of Jesuit Colleges and Universities.

Before being appointed university president, McShane was a dean of Fordham College at Rose Hill and president of the University of Scranton. He was ordained a priest in 1977.

A distinguished author, McShane won first prize from the Catholic Press Association in 1992. He is the author of the book *Sufficiently Radical: Catholicism, Progressivism, and the Bishops' Program of 1919,* as well as numerous articles, including "Roman Catholicism" in the *Encyclopedia Britannica Micropaedia.*

LIONEL NOWELL

Lionel L. Nowell III is senior vice president and treasurer of PepsiCo, Inc., a position he assumed in August 2001. He is responsible for the worldwide corporate treasury function, including worldwide financial activities, capital markets strategies, foreign exchange, and cash forecasting and planning.

With revenues of about $27 billion, PepsiCo ranks as the world's fourth-largest food and beverage company. It owns numerous companies and brands including Frito-Lay, the world's largest manufacturer and distributor of snacks; Pepsi-Cola, the second-largest soft drink business; Tropicana, the largest marketer and producer of branded juices; Gatorade, the world's leading sports drink; and Quaker Foods, which merged with PepsiCo in August 2001.

Previously, Nowell was chief financial officer for The Pepsi Bottling Group (PBG), a position he assumed in 2000. Before PBG, he was PepsiCo's controller. Nowell joined PepsiCo from RJR Nabisco, Inc., where he was senior vice president, strategy and business development. At RJR Nabisco, he played an active role in developing successful strategies to dramatically build shareholder value, including the sale of the company's international tobacco unit and spin-off of its domestic tobacco business.

Nowell is a member of the board of directors of American Electric Power Company, a $15 billion energy company based in Columbus, Ohio. He also is a member of the board of directors of Church & Dwight Co., a manufacturer and marketer of household, personal care, and specialty products under the Arm & Hammer trademark. He serves on the Dean's Advisory Council of Fisher College of Business at the Ohio State University and is an active member of the Executive Leadership Council, Financial Executive Institute, American Institute of Certified Public Accountants, and the Ohio Society of CPAs.

REVEREND JOSEPH O'HARE

Father Joseph O'Hare spent nineteen years as Fordham University's president, the longest tenure in university history. He was also the only person to have served as chairman to both the Association of Catholic Colleges and Universities and the Association of Jesuit Colleges and Universities.

O'Hare had an active role in the life of New York City as well, serving on the boards of several institutions and on a number of city commissions. In 1988, Mayor Ed Koch appointed him founding chairman of the New York City Campaign Finance Board, an agency that has since been hailed as a national model for campaign finance reform. He served in the position for fifteen years. In 1992, O'Hare was awarded the annual Civil Leadership Award, and he was honored by the Council on Governmental Ethics Laws (COGEL) in 1994 for distinguished achievement in the regulation of government ethics.

O'Hare taught for a number of years at a Jesuit university in the Philippines, returning to the States in 1972. He joined the editorial staff at *America,* the national Catholic weekly magazine, and went on to become the editor-in-chief until his appointment at

Fordham University in 1984. He is the recipient of nine honorary doctorates.

CHRISTINE POON

Christine Poon is a vice chairman of Johnson & Johnson; worldwide chairman, medicines and nutritionals; and a member of the office of the chairman. She serves as a member of J&J's executive committee and has responsibility for all pharmaceutical, consumer pharmaceutical, and nutritional businesses. In addition, the Nominating and Corporate Governance Committee of the Board of Directors nominated Poon for election to the board in April 2005.

Before joining Johnson & Johnson in November 2000, Poon spent fifteen years at Bristol-Myers Squibb Company, where her last position was as president of international medicines. Her career at Bristol-Myers Squibb included marketing and strategic planning. In 1990, she was named vice president, cardiovascular strategic product planning, and she became vice president and general manager of Squibb Diagnostics in 1992. In 1994, she was named president and general manager of the Canadian operation. She was later named vice president, then senior vice president, for Canada and Latin America pharmaceutical operations. From 1997 to 1998 she was president of medical devices for Bristol-Myers Squibb.

In 2004, Poon was named Woman of the Year by the Healthcare Businesswomen's Association.

FAITH POPCORN

Faith Popcorn, best-selling author of *Dictionary of the Future, EVEolution, Clicking,* and *The Popcorn Report,* is CEO of Faith

Popcorn's BrainReserve, the futurist marketing consultancy she founded in 1974. Recognized as America's foremost trends expert, she has identified such sweeping societal concepts as "cocooning," "cashing out," "anchoring," and "pleasure revenge."

As key strategist for BrainReserve, Popcorn applies her insights regarding cultural and business trends to help BrainReserve clients reposition established brands or companies, develop new products, and define areas of new business opportunity.

Documented as having a 95 percent accuracy rate, Popcorn correctly predicted consumer demand for fresh foods and four-wheel drives, as well as the spiritual tenor of the millennium (the anchoring trend). She was the first to anticipate the explosive growth in home delivery, home shopping, and home businesses (the armored cocoon). Her hour-long seminar, which focuses on how future trends affect consumer lifestyles and purchasing behavior, has been presented to thousands of audiences across the globe.

MYRTLE POTTER

Myrtle S. Potter joined Genentech Inc. in 2000 as executive vice president, chief operating officer, and a member of the executive committee. Potter leads Genentech's commercial operations, including sales, marketing, managed care, business development, commercial development, and decision support and commercial innovation functions. She also cochairs Genentech's Product Portfolio Committee, which is charged with providing strategic and financial oversight of the company's drug development portfolio.

Before joining Genentech, Potter was president of Bristol-Myers Squibb's U.S. Cardiovascular/Metabolics, a 3,000-person, multibillion-dollar business. Potter joined Bristol-Myers Squibb in

1996 as vice president of strategy and economics. She was promoted to vice president of the Worldwide Medicines Group, and then to senior vice president of sales for U.S. Cardiovascular/Metabolics, before becoming president of that business unit. Before joining Bristol-Myers, Potter spent fourteen years at Merck & Co. in a variety of sales, marketing, and business planning roles.

In 2002, *Time* magazine named Potter to its list of fifteen Young Global Business Influentials with especially promising and wide-reaching careers. Also in 2002, *Fortune* magazine featured Potter on its list of the most powerful black executives in America.

JEFF RICH

Jeff Rich is the leader of Affiliated Computer Services, Inc. (ACS). He joined ACS in July 1989 as senior vice president and chief financial officer. He has served as a director of ACS since 1991.

Rich is a young, energetic, highly competitive man of action. His passion for the business is evident from the moment you meet him. He possesses a strong affinity for his clients and enjoys interacting with them. And just like the company he runs, Rich is constantly establishing a vision, learning and growing to adapt to the world's changing marketplace.

Before joining ACS, he served as vice president of the Leverage Capital Group at Citibank N.A. He serves as a director of Pegasus Solutions, Inc., the United States Chamber of Commerce, and the Education Is Freedom Foundation. He serves on the Corporate Advisory Board of the University of Michigan Business School. He is currently chapter chairman of the Young Presidents' Organization and serves as a member of the Dallas Citizens Council. Rich contributes to several charitable organizations, including Best Buddies, AWARE, and the Body by Jake Foundation.

JIM ROBERTS

Jim Roberts is the executive director of AdvantageWest's Blue Ridge Entrepreneurial Council (BREC) and Blue Ridge Angel Investors Network (BRAIN). He has successfully launched and grown networks for Western North Carolina entrepreneurs and angel investors, providing education, mentoring, and capital formation and business plan preparation services to the groups' members and affiliates. BREC and BRAIN have been featured in *Entrepreneur*, the North Carolina Economic Development Guide, and the magazine of the International Economic Development Council.

Previously, Roberts served as the founder and CEO of First Round, an organization that promoted technology entrepreneurship and investment. He also was vice president of business development for Cydecor, a start-up web design company, and WebServe, an Internet service provider. When he was only thirty, Roberts was named one of the forty most influential people under age 40 by the *Charlotte Business Journal.*

HOWARD SAFIR

Howard Safir is chairman and CEO of SafirRosetti, an affiliate of the Omnicom Group Inc. SafirRosetti is a premier company serving the security and investigation needs of its clients both nationally and internationally. Safir also serves as consultant to the chair of

ChoicePoint, a leading provider of credential verification and identification services.

Safir was appointed thirty-ninth police commissioner of the City of New York by Mayor Rudolph W. Giuliani on April 15, 1996. In his four years as police commissioner, he achieved a 38 percent reduction in major crime and reduced homicides by 44 percent, bringing the total number of murders in New York to their lowest level in three decades. To obtain these results, Commissioner Safir implemented a comprehensive "fugitive strategy" and established thirty-nine major antidrug initiatives throughout the city.

To discourage the use of drugs among young people, Commissioner Safir introduced the largest Drug Abuse Resistance Education (DARE) program in the world, which has trained more than 220,000 students. He also introduced the Gang Resistance and Education Training Program, which has trained over 43,000 students to avoid gang activity.

As police commissioner, Safir took many steps to assist police officers and promote morale. He established commanders' days that allow commanding officers to recognize and reward the exceptional performance of subordinates by providing extra days off. He worked with lending institutions to arrange low-cost mortgages with no closing costs for officers purchasing residences within the city. He replaced 18,000 bullet-resistant vests, authorized the use of small off-duty 9mm firearms, expanded the police department's scholarship program, issued cellular phones to patrol supervisors, and established a portable defibrillator program to promote officers' and civilians' safety.

Safir began his law enforcement career in 1965 as a special agent assigned to the New York office of the Federal Bureau of Narcotics, a forerunner of the Drug Enforcement Administration (DEA). In 1977 he was appointed assistant director of the DEA. Safir also served as chief of the Witness Security Division of the

U.S. Marshals Service. He rejoined government service in 1994 when Mayor Giuliani asked him to serve as New York City's twenty-ninth fire commissioner.

Throughout his career, Safir has been recognized frequently for his outstanding service. He was twice awarded the Presidential Meritorious Executive Award. He has received the U.S. Marshals Service Meritorious Service Award and the Attorney General's Achievement Award, in addition to many other citations and honors.

BILL SHORE

Bill Shore is the founder and executive director of Share Our Strength, the nation's leading antihunger, antipoverty organization, which mobilizes industries and individuals to contribute their talents to fight hunger and poverty. Shore is also the chairman of Community Wealth Ventures, Inc., a for-profit subsidiary of Share Our Strength, which provides consulting services.

Shore founded Share Our Strength in 1984 in response to the Ethiopian famine and subsequently renewed concern about hunger in the United States. Since its founding, Share Our Strength has raised more than $188 million to support more than 1,000 antihunger, antipoverty groups worldwide. In 1997, Shore launched Community Wealth Ventures, Inc., to provide strategic counsel to corporations, foundations, and nonprofit organizations interested in creating community wealth—resources generated through profitable enterprise to promote social change.

From 1978 through 1987, Shore served on the senatorial and presidential campaign staffs of U.S. Senator Gary Hart (D-Colo.). From 1988 to 1991, he served as chief of staff for U.S. Senator

Robert Kerrey (D-Neb.). His transition from politics to innovative community service and his prescription for community change are documented in his first book, *Revolution of the Heart*. Shore's second book, *The Cathedral Within*, profiles a new breed of community leaders who are tapping every sector of society to improve community life. Shore's most recent book, *The Light of Conscience*, explores how acts of conscience can change and have changed the world.

Shore currently serves on the boards of directors of The Timberland Company, City Year, In2Books, College Summit, and Venture Philanthropy Partners. He also teaches a class on social entrepreneurship at New York University's Stern School of Business as an adjunct professor and has been a guest lecturer at the John F. Kennedy School of Government at Harvard University and at Stanford University's Graduate School of Business.

RANDY THURMAN

Randy Thurman is chairman, president, and CEO of VIASYS Healthcare, Inc., a global, research-based medical technology company that develops and markets respiratory, neurocare, and medical/surgical products. In early 2001, he led efforts to consolidate twenty-three independent companies before the company's subsequent public offering on the New York Stock Exchange. VIASYS has since become the world leader in respiratory and neurodiagnostics systems.

Before joining VIASYS Healthcare, Thurman was CEO of Strategic Reserves LLC and participated in a number of entrepreneurial ventures, including the start-up of two medical device companies and two genomics companies. As chairman of the board of Enzon Pharmaceuticals, Inc., he guided the company's growth from a $70 million market capitalization to over $2.5 billion. Previously, Thurman was chairman and CEO of Corning Life Sciences Inc., which under his leadership grew from $700 million to over $2 billion in revenue and subsequently was spun off as two NYSE companies.

Earlier in his career Thurman served as president of Rorer Pharmaceuticals and later Rhône-Poulenc Rorer. He also served as a United States Air Force combat pilot in Vietnam and subsequently as an instructor pilot in the USAF advanced jet program. He received the Distinguished Flying Cross and eight Air Medals for his service in combat.

BILL TOPPETA

William J. Toppeta is president of MetLife International, a role he's held since July 1, 2001. He is responsible for the company's insurance and employee benefits businesses outside the United States. Toppeta is also a member of MetLife's executive group, which he joined in 1997.

Under Toppeta's leadership, MetLife International has successfully expanded its operations into emerging markets with significant demand for insurance. As principal architect of MetLife's acquisition and integration of Aseguradora Hidalgo S.A., Toppeta has been instrumental in the creation of MetLife Mexico, the largest life insurer in that country.

Under Toppeta's direction, MetLife International's revenues more than doubled in three years—from $1.2 billion in 2001 to $2.5 billion in 2003. Likewise, the international customer base has grown significantly to 8 million in 2003. Toppeta continues to lead MetLife International to build its business organically and through opportunistic acquisitions, with specific focus on Latin America, Asia, and Europe.

Before assuming his current role, Toppeta held a series of leadership positions at MetLife. In 1999, he was appointed MetLife's president of client services and the company's chief administrative officer (CAO). Before that, Toppeta was head of the individual business segment in the United States, after having led the U.S. career agency force for three years. In 1995, he was appointed senior vice president to lead MetLife's corporate reengineering department.

Toppeta is an attorney and counselor at law in the state of New York, as well as a general securities principal and a chartered life underwriter.

BRUCE TULGAN

Bruce Tulgan is internationally recognized as one of the leading experts on young people in the workplace. Through his company, Rainmaker Thinking, he serves as an adviser to business leaders all over the world. The author of twelve books and numerous management training programs, Tulgan is also a sought-after keynote speaker and seminar leader.

Since 1995, Tulgan has addressed tens of thousands of leaders and managers in hundreds of organizations ranging from J. P. Morgan to J. C. Penney Company. He has been called "the new Tom Peters" by many who have seen him speak, and was named by *Management Today* as one of the few contemporary figures to stand out as a "management guru." His writings have appeared in numerous magazines and newspapers, including *Business Week,* the *New York Times,* the *Los Angeles Times,* and *USA TODAY.*

Before founding Rainmaker Thinking, Tulgan practiced law at the Wall Street firm of Carter, Ledyard & Milburn. He remains a member of the bar in Massachusetts and New York.

THOMAS VON ESSEN

Thomas Von Essen's courage and leadership helped the thirty-one-year veteran of the New York City Fire Department rise to the challenge of September 11, 2001. He stabilized the command structure of the fire department while coping with the unbearable losses of his members and their families. Commissioner Von Essen ensured that operations of the department continued throughout the city as he helped direct the largest rescue and recovery operation in New York City's history.

In 1996, Von Essen was appointed New York City's thirtieth fire commissioner. During his tenure, he secured $50 million to build a new, state-of-the-art fire training academy and instituted the first educational requirements for appointment and promotion. He expanded the specialty rescue units in response to the increased threat of bioterrorism and hazardous materials incidents, and expanded the training of the safety unit to increase oversight in the field. He secured extraordinary commitments from public and private sources that allowed the department to acquire the very latest equipment, including thermal imaging cameras and integrated personal alarm devices for every city firefighter. Von Essen created the Life Safety University to provide ongoing training for FDNY members and firefighters around the world. He also implemented the first Fire Cadet Program to recruit directly from city colleges and universities and increase the diversity of the department.

Von Essen is a *New York Times* best-selling author of *Strong of*

Heart. He served as president of the Uniformed Firefighters Association from 1993 until 1996. Since his retirement in 2001, Von Essen has been the senior vice president at Giuliani Partners and the chief executive officer of Giuliani–Von Essen LLC.

TERRY WACHALTER

Terry Wachalter joined Sander Flaum as a partner in Flaum Partners, Inc. in 2004. Formerly she served as executive vice president, director of global operations, for Euro RSCG Life and as executive vice president, operations, and CFO for Robert A. Becker Euro RSCG. Among her many successes, Wachalter pioneered, in 1997, the development and execution of a unique risk-sharing agreement with Bristol-Myers Squibb Company. This program was in force for its HIV brands and Tequin antibiotic for a number of years.

Even before most clients recognized the need for their own in-house marketing services function to purchase advertising agency services, Wachalter in 1998 became the indispensable partner of Wyeth in conceiving, developing, and executing a unique fee arrangement that solidified the client/agency partnership. She has been quoted in the *Wall Street Journal* and the *New York Times* and has appeared in an MSNBC segment on how to retain A+ people.

SOLA WINLEY

Sola Winley serves as the director of the Institute for Leadership and Change (ILC), an organization he created that is committed to strengthening the diversity of leadership within child welfare and human services. He also counsels teenagers and families in crisis for St. Christopher's, Inc., one of New York's oldest child welfare and social service agencies. Winley is also founder and CEO of ProVision Consulting Inc., a firm dedicated to assisting minority-owned businesses and professionals.

Before his work with ILC, Winley was a successful executive working with the National Football League's business divisions. He is a member of the National Black MBA Association, the New York State Society of Clinical Social Workers, the Black Psychiatrists of Greater New York, and the National Association of Social Workers.

GREG YOUNG

Gregory P. Young serves as CEO of CorePharma Holdings Inc., a leading developer and manufacturer of solid dose generic pharmaceuticals. Before joing CorePharma, he held the position of CEO and president of Neopharm, Inc., a start-up company focused on cancer research. Prior to that position Greg served as corporate vice president of Baxter Healthcare Corporation. He was president of Baxter's Transfusion Therapies (formerly known as Fenwal) business. The Transfusion Therapies business develops products and systems for the collection and processing of whole blood and blood components.

Young joined Baxter in 1985 and served in roles of increasing responsibility in sales, marketing, and product development within Baxter's medication delivery business. From 1996 to 1999 he served as president of the electronic infusion division. He assumed the position of president of Transfusion Therapies business in 1999 and corporate vice president in 2001.

Young is a member of the board of directors of the Lake Forest Graduate School of Management, a member of the University of Illinois at Chicago College of Pharmacy Advisory Committee, a trustee of the National Blood Foundation, and a member of the American Pharmaceutical Association.

INDEX

ABOUT THE
AUTHORS

Sander A. Flaum is a highly sought adviser to CEOs and executives and is the founder of Flaum Partners, a New York–based consultancy focused on transformational thinking for the pharmaceutical and biotech industries. He serves as adjunct professor of management at the Fordham Graduate School of Business, where he chairs the Fordham Leadership Forum. Sander also serves on the boards of Fisher College of Business at The Ohio State University, Fordham Graduate School of Business, Monterey Institute of International Studies, and VIASYS Healthcare.

Earlier in his career he was chairman and CEO of Robert A. Becker, Euro RSCG, a global advertising entity, where he led a global team of strategists who introduced and managed seven $2 billion brands.

Sander is a published author with over 40 articles to his credit on marketing, management, and leadership. His speaking credits include many keynote talks at pharmaceutical conferences and at domestic and international marketing congresses.

Sander received his undergraduate degree from The Ohio State University and his MBA from Fairleigh Dickinson University magna cum laude.

Jonathon A. Flaum is CEO of WriteMind Communications, Inc., an Asheville, North Carolina–based consultancy focused on compelling public communication and organizational creativity. Through the crafting of speeches, seminars, and workshops, WriteMind facilitates opportunities for organizations to explore the creative process that leads to innovation. Additionally, WriteMind works with corporate leaders to help them integrate their authentic personal voice with their business objectives when delivering a speech or presentation to their company/industry group or in preparing an article for publication.

In addition to his role as creative director for WriteMind, Jonathon serves as chief editorial consultant for the Louisiana State University Neuroscience Center of Excellence, where he creates public presentations, articles, and writings to aid staff in communication of their innovative scientific research to a lay audience. Jonathon holds an MA in philosophy of religion from Florida State University and an MFA in playwriting from the University of Southern California.

Mechele Flaum is the founder of Marketing Fire, a creative marketing consultancy with the mission of driving brands within a rapidly changing environment through identification and application of consumer trends. Marketing Fire has created profit- and share-winning strategies for packaged goods and business-to-business as well as consumer service concerns.

In her earlier career Mechele was president of Faith Popcorn's BrainReserve, where she spent more than a decade honing trend insights into product and marketplace strategies for companies such as American Home Products, Bell Atlantic, BMW, Chesebrough-Pond's, ConAgra, DAP, Dow Brands, Heublein, Hoffmann La-Roche, IBM, MetLife, Met-Rx, Pepsi-Lipton, RJR Nabisco, Rubbermaid, Seagram, Silicon Graphics, and The Burton Group, Ltd.

Mechele holds a BA from American University, an MA in American Folklore from the University of Pennsylvania, and an MBA from Columbia University Graduate School of Business. She is also on the editorial board of *Lifestyles* magazine and serves on the board of Brooklyn Friends School.

ATTN: CUSTOMER SERVICE

BUSINESS REPLY MAIL

FIRST-CLASS MAIL   PERMIT NO. 7172   NEW YORK, NY

POSTAGE WILL BE PAID BY ADDRESSEE

American Management Association
600 AMA WAY
SARANAC LAKE NY 12983-9963